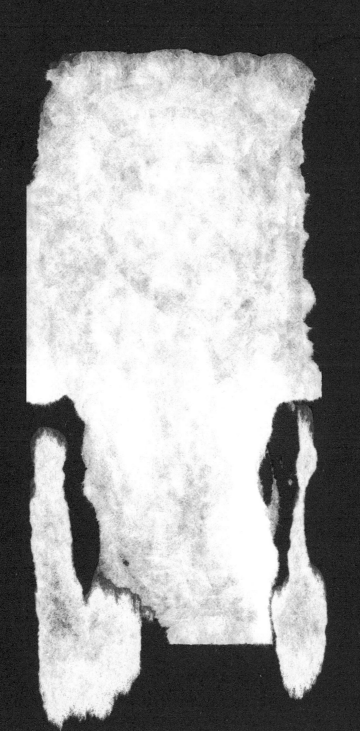

Golden Hands Encyclopedia of

CRAFTS

Marshall Cavendish

Contents

∗ Not suitable for children without adult supervision

Suppliers addresses United Kingdom

Please send a s.a.e. with any enquiries to the suppliers below

Paint 24. Leichner theatrical make-up at Charles H. Fox Ltd, 25 Shelton St, London WC2H 9HX and good chemists and department stores.

Paint 25. Gilding requisites at E Ploton (Sundries) Ltd, 273 Archway Road, London N6 5AA who also offer mail order service and catalogue.

Paint 26. Hand coloured photographs from Susan Wilks, 70 Latchmere Rd, London SW11. Photo Oil colours by Winsor & Newton Ltd, 51 Rathbone Place, London W1P 1AB. All necessary chemicals for photo colouring at Rayco Instruments Ltd, Blackwater Way, Ash Rd, Aldershot, Hants.

Clay 39. Materials at The Fulham Pottery Ltd, 210 New King's Rd, London SW6 4NY or at Southern Supplies Centre, 42 Morley Rd, Tonbridge, Kent; Harrison Mayer Ltd, Meir, Stoke-on-Trent ST3 7PX (who also sell felt tipped pens); Ferro (Great Britain) Ltd, Wombourne, Wolverhampton WV5 8DA who also supply overseas; Wengers Ltd, Garner St, Etruria, Stoke-on-Trent, Staffs ST4 7BQ.

Clay 40. Materials at The Fulham Pottery Ltd, 210 New King's Rd, London SW6 4NY and at Southern Supplies Centre, 42 Morley Road, Tonbridge, Kent; Harrison Mayer Ltd, Meir, Stoke-on-Trent, Staffs ST3 7PX; Ferro (Great Britain) Ltd, Wombourne, Wolverhampton WV5 8DA who also supply overseas; Wengers Ltd, Garner St, Etruria, Stoke-on-Trent, Staffs ST4 7BQ. Commercial tile cutter at Podmore & Sons Ltd, Shelton, Stoke-on-Trent, Staffs who also offer mail order service and Ferro (Great Britain) Ltd.

Clay 41. A wide range of clay requisites at Clayglaze, Kings Yard, Talbot Rd, Rickmansworth, Herts. Clay tools at H W Anger & Son Ltd, 1 Mill Lane, Polstead, Colchester CO6 5AB. (Both addresses also offer mail order service). For further clay addresses see Clay chapter 40, above. Napkin, china and fabric (in background) at Habitat, 206 King's Rd, London SW3 and branches.

Clay 42. Materials at The Fulham Pottery Ltd, 210 New King's Rd, London SW6 4NY or at Southern Supplies Centre, 42 Morley Rd, Tonbridge, Kent; Harrison Mayer Ltd, Meir, Stoke-on-Trent, Staffs ST3 7PX; Ferro (Great Britain) Ltd, Wombourne, Wolverhampton WV5 8DA who also supply overseas; Wengers Ltd, Garner St, Etruria, Stoke-on-Trent, Staffs ST4 7BQ.

Sewing 23. Materials at John Lewis, 278 Oxford St, London W1A 1EX and branches.

Metal 24. The following addresses also offer mail order service. Kits at Lapidary Abrasives, 12a Old Balshaw's Yard, Market St, Altrincham, Cheshire and Crafts & Kilns, 376 Finchley Rd, London NW3 7AJ. Student's alloy at Cottrell & Co, Precious Metals Dept, 15 Charlotte St, London W1P 2AA.

Metal 25. The following addresses also offer mail order service. Kits at Lapidary Abrasives, Old Balshaw's Yard, 12A Market St, Altrincham, Cheshire and Crafts & Kilns, 376 Finchley Rd, London NW3 7AJ. Student's alloy at Cottrell & Co, Precious Metal Dept, 15 Charlotte St, London W1P 2AA. Finishes at Expo (Drills) Ltd, Unit 5A, Sustanum Works, Titchfield, Hants.

Metal 26. A wide range of silver wire, tubing and sheeting is available at J Blundell & Sons Ltd, 199 Wardour St, London W1V 4JN who also offer mail order service; Johnson Matthey Metals Ltd, Victoria St, Birmingham B1 3MZ for mail order only and 100 High St, Southgate, London N14 6ET for personal shoppers.

Weaving 22. Looms at Harris Looms, Northgrove Rd, Hawkshurst, Kent TN18 4AP who also offer mail order service and catalogue.

Weaving 23. Botany wool at Dryad, PO Box 38, Northgates, Leicester, Leics LE1 9BU (mail order only) and at Reeves Dryad Shop, 178 Kensington High St, London W8 for personal shoppers. Looms and accessories at Harris Looms, Northgrove Rd, Hawkhurst, Kent TN18 4AP who also offer mail order service and catalogue. Shooting stick and binoculars from Moss Bros, Bedford St, London WC2E 8JB. Scarf and bangles from John Lewis, 278 Oxford St, London W1A 1EX.

Paper 47. Mounting board and other materials at craft shops and stationers.

Paper 49. Balsa wood at hardware, DIY and craft shops.

Upholstery 10. Foam at Grant Baxell, 195A Upper Richmond Rd, London SW15 who also offer mail order service. Curtaining and upholstery fabrics by G P & J Baker Ltd, 28 Berners St, London W1P 4NA.

Upholstery 11. Materials at Grant Baxell, 195A Upper Richmond Rd, London SW15. Bedspread at Habitat (see under Clay).

Upholstery 12. Upholstery materials from Grant Baxell, 195a Upper Richmond Rd, Putney, London SW15. Blouse at Laura Ashley, 9 Harriet St, London SW1.

Paint 27. Artist's watercolours by mail order from Reeves, PO Box 48, 249 Lincoln Rd, Enfield, Middx 1SX and Winsor & Newton, 51 Rathbone Pl, London W1P 1AB for personal shoppers and mail order service. Wallpaper at Laura Ashley, 40 Sloane St, London SW1. Engravings framed by Blackman Harvey Ltd, 29/39 Earlham St, London WC2.

Finishes 6. Veneers available at Crispin's, 94 Curtain Rd, London EC2A 3AA who also offer mail order service. Other equipment at DIY and hardware stores.

Fur 1. Rabbit skins and mink tails at A. L. Mangham, 5 Fazakerley St, Liverpool, Lancs, W3 9DN. Selection of furs and rabbit fur coat at Boutique Furs Manufacturing Ltd, 22 Barrett St, London W1. Bedspread at Harrods, Knightsbridge, London SW1 and Peter Jones, Sloane Sq, London SW1. Beret by Kangol.

Metrication

In this volume you will find two systems of measurement. The first set of figures refers to the metric system and the Imperial figures follow in brackets. Wherever possible, a commonsense approach has been adopted and both sets of measurements have been worked out in round numbers. **BUT BEWARE!** This means that metric and the Imperial figures are *not* equivalent so make sure you only work with one or other set of figures.

This edition published 1980

© Marshall Cavendish Ltd, MCMLXXVI 58, Old Compton Street, London, W1V 5PA

Golden Hands is The Trademark of Western Publishing Company Inc. and the use hereof by Marshall Cavendish is by licence.

Printed and bound in Singapore by Tien Wah Press (Pte) Ltd

Creative ideas 64

Side-table setting
Here is a pretty setting which was inspired by an attractive print of a flower arrangement. The print may have been discovered after many pleasurable hours spent browsing around antique shops, or it may have been a forgotten heirloom in the attic.

By studying the style of the print the designer has interpreted it in a three-dimensional table display. In this case a cup and saucer similar in shape were found. Then appropriate flowers were arranged to repeat the picture's shape and form—the artist's still life is thus given new dimensions.

By carefully adding more flowers and other decorative items an eye-catching side-table setting has been created.

An idea inspired by, and then created from, a print.

Jessica Strang

Faces for footlights

A young model, surrounded by a vast array of theatrical make-up, before she starts to turn herself into an old lady.

Melvin Grey

Professional make-up for the theatre is the essential equipment with which an actor is able to adjust, or if necessary completely alter, his skin colour and features so that he resembles the character he is portraying. A bolder emphasis of features with make-up may be necessary in the larger halls and theatres so that under all conditions of lighting and distance from the stage as many people as possible in the audience can see and believe in the character. In general, the heavily made-up look is to be avoided—the appearance should be as natural as possible to be acceptable to modern audiences. Leading professional and amateur actors make a careful study of this art because they are aware of the enormous psychological boost they get from a well planned and carefully applied make-up. If they walk on stage satisfied that they look in character they will feel in character and play with greater confidence.

The effects of lighting

The lighting in the dressing room is never the same as that used to light the stage in so far as the colour and power of the light is concerned, therefore it is advisable for a 'make-up parade' to be held on stage before the dress rehearsal so that the appearance can be checked by the director and an adjustment made before the entertainment actually gets under way.

The effect of very intense light is to drain colour from the skin, and this is easy to counteract by using the darker shades of make-up.

Coloured light. Colour filters are used by directors to suit the particular requirements of the entertainment—mood, atmosphere, season of the year, time of day etc—and the actor quickly realizes that while the effect of the colour filters on make-up and costume can often be flattering, sometimes they can give the reverse effect.

The soft, gentle colour filters such as straw, rose, salmon and gold very often enhance the appearance but those such as deep amber and yellow tend to drain subtle red tints from the skin, giving a sallow, flat yellowish effect. The mid-pink and peach shades tend to lose their brightness and liveliness and the light tan appears very much darker.

In general when the colour of the filter is predominantly red, it will drain any pink or red from the foundation, cheeks and lips and this could be adjusted by using the darker tones of red. Under these filters the greens, blues and mauves often used as eye shadows by women will darken and it may be necessary to choose the lighter tones of these shades.

Any excessive green in the lighting will have the reverse effect to this, and therefore the red in the foundation, cheeks and lips might have to be lightened, and the eye shadow darkened.

Under predominantly blue light the redness in the make-up would tend to take on a purplish tint making it necessary to use beige tinted foundation and the more brownish tints of lipstick and cheek colouring.

All this may seem to add a tedious, annoying, as well as highly technical complication to making up but, with observation and practice, a good working knowledge of the correct shades to use to counteract any adverse effects of lighting colour filters can be acquired fairly quickly.

Position of lights. Another effect which is well worth considering is that when the stage is flooded with an even intensity of light from above the stage and the wings, the highlights and shadows which give shape to the face sometimes become neutralized. The result is a rather flat appearance.

Highlights and shadows may therefore have to be added with make-up to restore the natural contours of the face. Fortunately directional spotlights and floodlights are being used with great imagination by lighting designers today and often it is not necessary to make great alteration with make-up.

Standard face make-up

Greasepaint should be applied to a clean skin which is absolutely free from greasiness. Men may wash with soap and water. Girls should remove their day-time make-up by gently massaging with a removing cream and wiping away with tissues. If there is still a film of cream remaining on the skin, this should be removed with astringent lotion or skin freshener on damp cotton wool. Next give the face a light application of foundation as described in Paint chapter 23, page 1728, blending in the colour at the hairline and smoothing it out well down the neck. Pat to a smooth even surface with the fingers, and then blot with a tissue to remove any surplus.

Remember there is sufficient depth and density of pigment in the greasepaint to ensure that only a light film of foundation is necessary to give maximum covering effect and the skin can therefore be tinted without obliterating skin texture.

Next it may be necessary to add cheek tints as well as highlighting and shading to counteract any flattening effects of stage lighting.

Cheeks. The positioning of cheek tint is most important. Various shades are available, ranging from the pinks through the bright reds to the coral or brownish reds. As the human eye will travel very quickly to red, it should become apparent that the positioning of the cheek tint can help to alter the shape of the face.

The centre of the cheeks is usually the main position of cheek tint. If, however, the face is too round, cheek tint should be smoothed on high along the line of the cheek-bone towards the temples. This can be further accentuated by placing a highlight on the top of the cheek-bone and a shadow immediately below (fig.1).

If the face is too thin, cheek tint should be applied from centre of cheek and smoothed out towards ear. Add a highlight on top of the cheek-bone fading out towards side of face (fig.2).

Carmine shades (red) for women's cheeks and brick red for men are generally the most effective.

Lips. Here, too, carmine shades are mainly used for women; and for men brick red (sometimes outlined with dark carmine or crimson lake) is suitable.

It is essential that the lip colour should not smudge if touched. The correct method of application is first to dry the lips by wiping with a tissue and then paint on the lip colour to the shape required with a lip-brush or directly from the stick. Blot the lips with a tissue, powder with rose blending powder and finally dab with damp cotton wool.

Alterations can be made to the shape of the lips by the careful application of make-up. Lips can be made fuller by broadening the shape with lipstick and then painting a thin outline around them with ivory highlight. If the lips are too thick, paint them to the narrower shape required and carry the foundation shade of make-up right up to the new line of the lips.

To shorten a wide mouth do not apply lipstick to the full width of the mouth but increase the depth.

Eyes. The eyes are the most expressive part of the face, and the object is to enlarge them and make them stand out. Over-emphasis will only close them up. Unfortunately, with distance in the theatre, the eye tends to disappear because the whites of the eyes tend to merge with the skin tone around them. By shading around them so that they are clearly outlined, they can be seen distinctly quite a long way from the stage.

First apply eyeshadow to the upper eyelid (men are advised to use mainly the brown shades), fading it upwards and outwards. Add a touch of a darker shade than that of the foundation (golden tan or brick red is suitable) to the eye hollow immediately above the eyelid, fading it upwards to the eyebrow, unless the eyes are very deep set, in which case use a lighter shade than the foundation.

With a brown or black wax pencil such as Leichner's Spot-Lite pencil draw a thin line under the extended eyeshadow from outer corner of upper eyelids sloping upwards and outwards (fig.3). With the same pencil draw a line immediately beneath the lower lashes. Colour eyebrows where necessary with a Spot-Lite pencil, sharpened to a fine point, applying the colour with a series of thin lines, to represent hair, rather than with one thick line. Use mascara on the eyelashes.

The finishing touch. Finally, the completed make-up should be powdered with rose blending powder. Use a velour puff for this purpose and then brush off any surplus powder from skin.

Highlights and shadows

The contours of a face can be changed considerably with the subtle use of make-up but it is emphasized that make-up should fit in with the actor's own facial structure so that any movement caused by natural expression does not look artificial.

Highlights (ivory or white) are used to bring features into prominence;

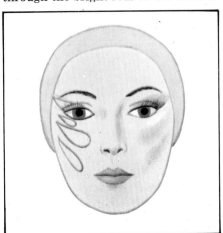

1. *Round face. Left side: areas for colour. Right side: make-up completed.*

2. *Thin face. Left side: areas for colour. Right side: completed make-up.*

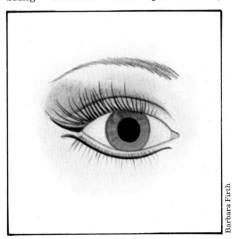

Barbara Firth

3. *Eye made up to stand out when viewed from a distance.*

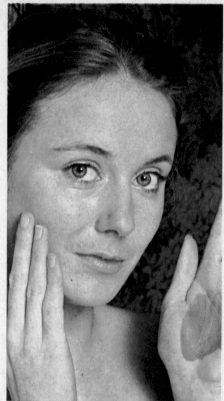

Sallow foundation containing pink undertone. Rub stick on to palm of one hand, rub hands together and apply foundation to face with one or both hands.

Shade sides of forehead and highlight lips. Use highlights and shadows in conjunction under bottom lip and on chin and to make 'folds' on forehead.

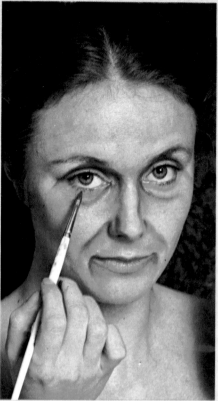

Fade back eye by applying shadows to eye-hollow and cheek-bone and highlighting the bone and above eyebrow.

Highlight above upper lip and create pouches under eyes. When applying shading use a brush and soften by patting with finger-tips.

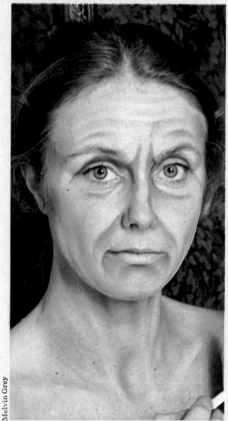

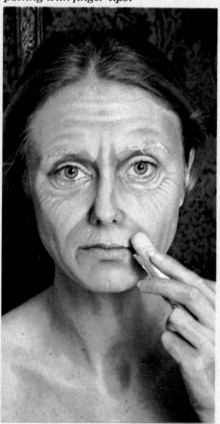

shadows, or lowlights (deep brown greasepaint), do the reverse. Both are used in conjunction with one another. As a simple example the effect of sunken cheeks can be simulated, in conjunction with correctly placed cheek tints, by shading immediately beneath the cheek-bone, fading the colour downwards and highlighting above the bone with ivory highlight. Shading the sides of the forehead will make it appear narrower while highlighting the sides will broaden it.

It is very simple to make alterations to the shape of the nose. A very broad nose can be made thinner by placing shadows high up on the bridge at the sides and running down the length of the nose. Shadows placed lower down the bridge of the nose will broaden it, while a shadow placed underneath the tip will shorten it.

Ageing

Highlighting and shading is used to give the impression of age by simulating the ageing folds of skin.

In a smooth young face there is less contrast of highlight and shadow than in an older one where the shadows and highlights are much sharper. This type of make-up is achieved by concentrating on the highlighting rather than the shading. Before applying highlights and shadows, sit in front of a mirror and move the features in various expressions so that you can clearly see where the natural shadows and highlights are going to occur with age. Then apply the shading material (deep brown greasepaint) to the required position with the tip of the little finger. Smooth out the shadow with the fingers, away from the deepest point of indentation. Take an ivory or white highlighting shade and apply above the shadows, smoothing out the highlight into the foundation shade.

In this way the deepest point of the highlight will be above the deepest point of the shadow—both gradually fading outwards into the foundation shade. The total effect is to give the illusion of folds of flesh and not thin lines on a flat skin surface.

Only the method of ageing a face has so far been mentioned but, obviously, all flesh parts that show—neck, arms and particularly the backs of hands—must be made up in character. It is pointless ageing the face if, when a gesture brings the hands close to the face, they are seen to be young. The same broad method of shading and highlighting is used on these parts of the body as on the face.

Right: made-up hands and crepe hair complete the ageing process. Deep brown and a little crimson lake is used with ivory highlight.

A cottage candle holder

The cottage in place over a night-light, which must stand in water for safety. The friendly glow from the windows brings comfort to a darkened room.

Set of felt-tipped underglaze colours.
Clear glaze.
Two boards.
Fine brush and plate.

☐ First of all read the section on slab pot techniques in Clay chapter 20, page 874.

☐ Enlarge and cut out a paper pattern following the design below.

☐ Roll out a slab with an even thickness of about 6mm (¼″).

☐ Starting with the base, place the pattern pieces on the rolled clay and cut around them with the sharp knife. Use the ruler as a guide to ensure straight sides where necessary. Cut out the hole for the night-light.

☐ When all the pieces have been cut out, allow the clay to stiffen to the leather-hard stage.

☐ Place the base on a board (for easy

This little clay cottage was inspired by the famous Coalport cottages that have long been antique collectors' items. Yet the construction is so simple that even a beginner could make it, using cut slabs, rolled coils and sieved clay. A hole is cut in the base so that the cottage can be placed over a lighted night-light candle, and the chimney is strictly functional because it emits the resulting smoke. The cottage is decorated with instant felt-tipped underglaze colours prior to firing.

Making the cottage
You will need:
About 2kg (4 lb) of prepared clay.
About ½kg (1 lb) wet clay for sieving.
Thick paper for the pattern.
Pencil.
Ruler.
Rolling pin.
Sharp knife.
Clay tools for decoration.
Thick slip.
Fine-mesh nylon sieve.
Palette knife or spatula.

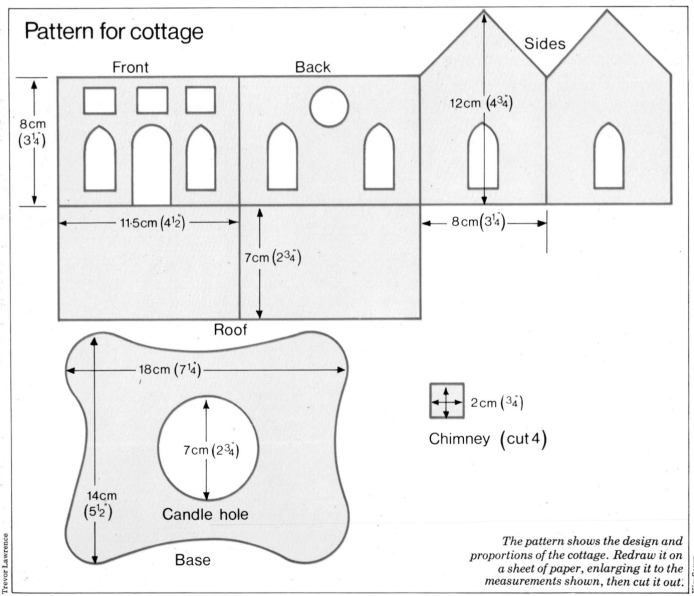

Pattern for cottage

Front   Back   Sides

8cm (3¼″)

12cm (4¾)

11·5cm (4½″)

8cm (3¼″)

7cm (2¾″)

Roof

18cm (7¼)

7cm (2¾″)
Candle hole

14cm (5½″)

Base

2cm (¾″)

Chimney (cut 4)

The pattern shows the design and proportions of the cottage. Redraw it on a sheet of paper, enlarging it to the measurements shown, then cut it out.

Trevor Lawrence

Kim Sayer

turning when decorating) and attach the walls to it, and to each other, with a generous coating of thick slip.

The latticed windows. These must be added from inside the cottage before the roof is put on.

☐ Use the left-over pieces of clay to roll out 15 coils, each about 6mm ($\frac{1}{4}''$) longer than the width of the window for which they are intended.

☐ Pinch both ends of each coil, to flatten them.

☐ Arrange the coils as shown across each window from the inside, and use slip to attach the flattened ends to the inside walls (fig.1).

Roof. When the walls have dried out sufficiently to take the weight of the roof, fix it in place, using plenty of slip and making sure that there are no gaps between it and the walls.

Chimney. Using the sharp knife, cut a square about 2cm x 2cm ($\frac{3}{4}''$x $\frac{3}{4}''$) out of the centre of the roof.

☐ For the chimney itself, use the **four** small squares already cut out, measuring to ensure that they will fill the hole when joined together with slip.

☐ Fix the chimney in place with slip, smoothing the join between it and the roof with your fingertips.

Decorating the cottage
Coil decoration
☐ Roll out some coils about 6mm ($\frac{1}{4}''$) thick and cut off lengths as required

for the ridge pole of the roof, window-sills, doorway and the beams under the eaves at the sides.

☐ Flatten them slightly and attach them with slip.

☐ The ridge pole should be attached in two lengths, from the chimney to the edge of the roof in each direction. Attach it with slip and mould it slightly into the roof.

☐ Cut four circles from a coil and apply one to each end of the ridge pole and one above each of the lower front windows. Use a clay-decorating tool to apply the 'rosette' pattern.

The finished cottage, biscuit-fired and ready for the application of colour.

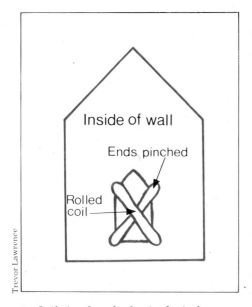

1. *Coils in place for latticed windows.*

☐ Texture and patterns can be applied to the coils and to the roof with wooden clay-decorating tools.

Sieved decoration

Sieving is an easy but effective technique which can be used to decorate many different models or pots. It can be used for thatched roofs, grass, the foliage of trees and bushes, animal fur or human hair. In fact it can be used anywhere that you want to add an interesting depth of texture. On this cottage it is used for the hedge border.

☐ Place the wet clay in the sieve and simply push it through the mesh with your thumbs, laying it along a board as it squiggles through.

It is a good idea to experiment with the consistency of the clay until a fairly stiffish paste is achieved—one that presses through well.

☐ Leave the sieved clay to dry out to a leather-hard consistency, for ease of handling, and then take it off the board with the palette knife, taking care not to squash the texture.

☐ Attach the sieved clay to the model with slip.

When the clay decoration is in place, the cottage is ready to be biscuit-fired, as shown in the picture, before the colour is added.

Felt-tipped underglaze colours

These pens can be used on biscuit-fired pottery and then glazed with a clear glaze. They are useful for someone who wants a range of colours without complicated mixing, mess or wastage, and they also give a professional finish for someone who is not very confident with a brush; but unfortunately these pens are rather expensive.

It is wise to work on a trial piece, to get the feel of the pens, before decorating the cottage itself.

Remember to press the tip of the pen down hard on the working surface to

make the colour flow. The tip should come out when you lift the pen up, but if it jams the colour will blot, so pull the felt tip out again if necessary.

Should a mistake occur it can be scratched off with a sharp knife after the colour has dried slightly.

Keep the decoration simple, as the tips are not very fine, and go over each line at least twice to ensure good colour transference.

Any difficult corners or fine bits of decoration can be filled in by pumping some of the colour out of the pen on to a plate—by pressing the pen down hard several times—and then using a fine brush to apply it to the cottage. Take care not to smudge the colours while applying the decoration (they tend to rub off until glazed).

This particular cottage was decorated with brown for the roof, black for roof edge and chimney edge and front path, blue for the latticed windows and pink for the surrounding hedge, but nine different colours are available so a

The cottage also makes an attractive and unusual table decoration.

wide range of decoration is possible—realistic or fanciful.

When the cottage is decorated, 'fire on' the colours before glazing by heating to approximately 600° to 650°C (1112° to 1202°F). This burns out any organic media in the colours that could reject the glaze.

Glazing

To avoid smudging the decoration the cottage should either be dipped in the glaze or else spray-glazed.

The pens can also be used on unfired glaze to give in-glaze colours.

Firing

The firing range of each colour is marked on the pen, and varies from 1080°C to 1250°C (1976°F to 2282°F). In this case the pink, at the lowest end of the range, and the blue, at the highest, were both used and a mid-way temperature of 1150°C (2102°F) produced satisfactory results.

Four-piece duvet set

Cloth — sewing 23

A duvet set dispenses with the need for a bedspread and can be made in matching or complimentary colours.

Duvets or continental quilts are an increasingly popular form of bedding, devised from the warm feather beds characteristic of Germany and Eastern European countries. These quilts not only replace the top sheet and blankets, but they are easy to handle, light to sleep under and retain heat exceptionally well. Duvets are available with a number of different stuffings: goose down, feathers and a mixture of feathers and down; also synthetics such as polyester mixtures. Of these, pure down is the most superior but all will give a warm comfortable covering. Because of their simple rectangular shape, it is very easy to make a duvet cover and less expensive than buying one. A complete matching set comprised of valance, bottom sheet, pillowcase and duvet cover can be made.

There are many interesting ways of making the set attractive and individual: plain or printed fabrics can be used or appliqué worked using a motif from the curtains. Alternating panels of contrasting fabrics could also be used.

Bed sizes

Quantities and instructions are for two standard sizes of bed.

Single bed size: 90cm x 190cm (3′x 6′3″).

Small double bed size: 135cm x 190cm (4′6″x 6′3″).

Individual quantities are given for each piece of the set, made from either 178cm (70″) wide sheeting for a single size, or 228cm (90″) wide sheeting for a double size.

Sheeting in a polyester and cotton mixture is preferable as it is quick drying and requires little or no ironing. Unless otherwise stated, instructions given are the same for a single bed or

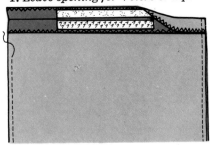

1. Leave opening for Velcro or zip.

2. Stitch fastening into opening.

double bed, the base standing 30cm (12″) from the floor.

1.5cm (½″) turnings have been allowed unless otherwise stated.

Duvet cover

Size: the average size of a duvet is 137cm x 198cm (54″x 78″) for a single bed and 198cm x 198cm (78″x 78″) for a small double bed.

The duvet cover should be about 5cm (2″) larger all round than the duvet. This enables the duvet to move freely inside the cover.

There are various ways of fastening the cover, but the easiest and most popular are Velcro or a zip fastener.

You will need:

Single duvet cover: 4.30m (4⅝yd) of 178cm (70″) wide fabric.

1m (40″) of 2cm (¾″) wide Velcro or 75cm (30″) zip fastener.

Matching thread.

Double duvet cover: 4.30m (4⅝yd) of 228cm (90″) wide fabric.

1m (40″) of 2cm (¾″) wide Velcro or 75cm (30″) zip fastener.

Matching thread.

Cutting out

☐ For a single cover cut two rectangles 150cm x 211cm (59″x 83″).

☐ For a double cover cut two rectangles 211cm x 211cm (83″x 83″).

Making up

☐ First prepare the bottom end of the cover to take the Velcro or zip.

☐ Neaten with a zigzag stitch the two raw edges and turn 2.5cm (1″) to the wrong side and press.

☐ With right sides facing, stitch these two edges of the duvet cover together along this crease line leaving an opening in the centre of the seam the length of the Velcro or zip (fig.1).

☐ Insert the zip into the opening or stitch the Velcro to each side of the opening (fig.2).

☐ Press the turnings open for a zip or to one side if using Velcro.

☐ With right sides facing, stitch the remaining three sides together taking 1.5cm (½″) turnings. Trim the turnings at the corners and neaten them together with a zigzag stitch.

☐ Turn the cover through to the right side and press lightly.

Fitted bottom sheet

A fitted bottom sheet with elastic corners will fit neatly over the mattress and will not slip out of position; it will also crease less than a plain unfitted sheet.

You will need:

2.75m (3yd) of 178cm (70″) wide fabric for single and 228cm (90″) for double bed size.

1m (40″) of 1.5cm (½″) wide elastic.

Matching thread.

Cutting out

☐ Cut a rectangle of fabric to the size

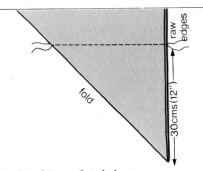

3. Stitching a fitted sheet corner.

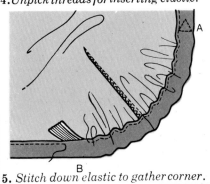

4. Unpick threads for inserting elastic.

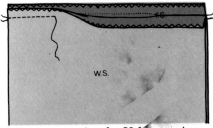

5. Stitch down elastic to gather corner.

of the mattress plus 38cm (15″) all round. The figures allow for an easy fit.

Making up

☐ With right sides facing, fold each corner of the rectangle so that the raw edges lie together on top of each other forming a point.

☐ Stitch across the corner 30cm (12″) from the point (fig.3).

☐ Cut off the point to within 5mm (¼″) of the stitching line and neaten the raw edges together with a zigzag stitch.

☐ Work a small hem all around the outside edge of the sheet; first turn under 5mm (¼″) and then 2cm (¾″). Machine stitch close to the fold.

☐ At each corner measure off 25cm (10″) to each side of the dart; this section will form a channel for the elastic. Upick a few stitches at each point, A and B (fig.4). Cut a 25cm (10″) length of elastic and thread through the channel from A to B. Secure the ends of the elastic by stitching small triangles over each end, through all thicknesses (fig.5). Stitch the opening. Press.

☐ Repeat with the other three corners then fit the sheet over the mattress.

Valance

The valance is a frill of fabric attached to a rectangle of matching fabric or calico, and placed under the mattress so that the frill hangs to the floor, covering the base of the bed and the legs.

The length of the frill should be about double the three sides of the bed, unless you wish the frill to go all around in which case it would be double the four sides of the bed.

You will need:

For a valance which goes round three sides 30.5cm (12″) finished depth:

4m (4½yd) of 178cm (70″) fabric for single bed.

4m (4½yd) of 228cm (90″) fabric for double bed.

3m (3yd) of 1.5cm (½″) wide tape for ties.

Cutting out

Remember that 1.5cm (½″) turnings are allowed throughout.

☐ First cut a rectangle of fabric to fit the top of the bed, plus 1.5cm (½″) all round.

☐ For the frill cut 6 strips of fabric each from the full width of the fabric 33.5cm (13½″) deep.

Making up

☐ With right sides facing, stitch the frill pieces together into one long strip. Neaten raw edges together with a zigzag stitch and press to one side.

☐ Trim frill to the required length.

☐ Work a small double hem taking 1.5cm (½″) along one long edge of the frill (this is the bottom of the frill) and across the two short ends, mitring corners.

☐ Divide the frill into eight equal parts along the remaining long edge (fig.6).

☐ Work two rows of gathering through each section.

Attaching the frill to the base.

Neaten the top end of the base cover with a small 1.5cm (½″) hem.

☐ Measure and divide the remaining three sides of the base cover into eight equal parts and mark with pins.

☐ With right sides facing, gather and pin the frill to the base cover, matching the pins on the frill to the pins on the base cover (fig.7). Pull up the gathering threads and distribute the fullness evenly. Tack and stitch. Neaten the turnings together with a zigzag stitch and press towards the frill (fig.8).

For a strong finish and to make sure the frill hangs correctly you can add another row of stitches. Work from

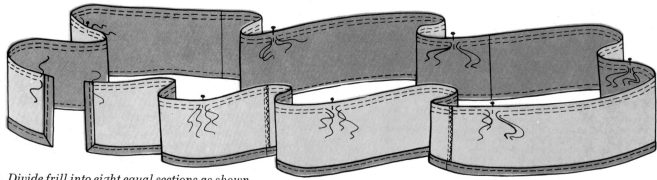

6. *Divide frill into eight equal sections as shown.*

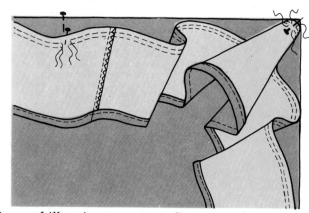

7. *Connect frill sections to corresponding top sections.*

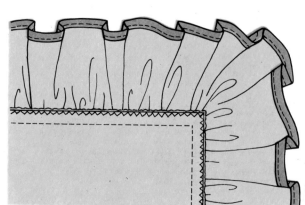

8. *Press gathered seam towards frill.*

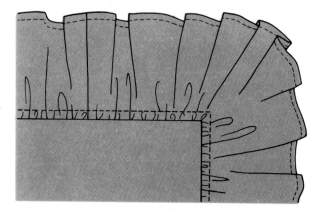

9. *Topstitching through all thicknesses is optional.*

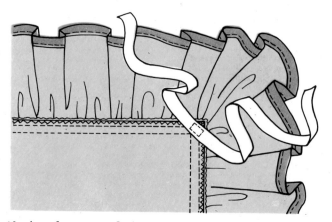

10. *Attach tape to valance corners. Tie these to posts.*

Coral Mula

Steve Bicknell

Lightweight duvet with colourful covers makes a welcoming bed!

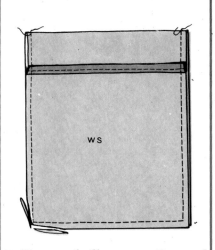

11. *Hem top of pillowcase sections and then sew sections together.*

larger rectangle by stitching a small double hem, taking 1.5cm ($\frac{1}{2}''$) turnings.

☐ Make a 1.5cm ($\frac{1}{2}''$) double hem on one short edge of the smaller rectangle.

☐ With right sides facing, place the two rectangles together with raw edges level. Fold the extending flap on the larger piece down over the smaller piece as shown (fig.11).

☐ With right sides facing, stitch the two rectangles together on three sides, leaving the finished ends open.

☐ Trim the turnings at the corners and neaten the raw edges together with a zigzag stitch.

☐ Turn the pillowcase to the right side and fold flap to the inside.

right side and tack the frill through seam allowance through all thicknesses. Then with one edge of the machine foot to the stitching line, stitch through all thicknesses (fig.9).

☐ Cut the tape into four equal lengths and stitch the centre of each piece to a corner of the valance on the wrong side as indicated (fig.10).

☐ Place the completed valance on the base under the mattress and tie the tapes around the legs of the bed, under the frill.

Pillowcase

For a pillow about 70cm x 50cm (27″ x 19″)
You will need:
70cm ($\frac{3}{4}$yd) of 178cm (70″) wide fabric.
Cutting out
☐ Cut out two rectangles, one measuring 89cm x 55cm ($34\frac{1}{2}''$ x 21″) and the other 75cm x 55cm (29″ x 21″).
Making up
☐ First neaten one short edge of the

Right: detail shows neatly fitted corners and completed valance.

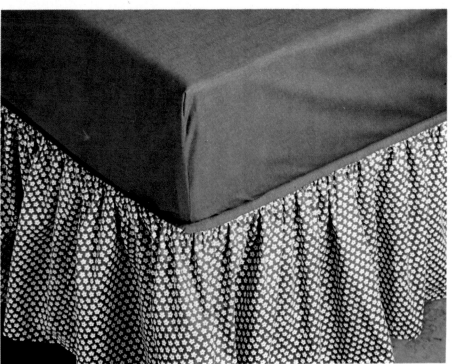

Introducing lost wax casting

Lost wax casting or *cire perdue*—the French term meaning lost wax—is the name given to a method of metal casting whose origins have been lost in history. Basically, the process involves making a model in wax of the object to be cast, then building a mould around it. The wax is later 'burnt-out' or 'lost'.

Known since the Bronze Age, lost wax casting gave early artists and crafts-men extraordinary freedom to create beautiful objects in intractable metals. Many of the world's most famous statues have been made with this process and examples survive from ancient Greece, Rome and early African cultures.

Before the 20th century, however, lost wax casting was rarely used for making fine ornaments or jewelry—the laborious techniques were reserved for statuary and work of a monumental nature. But in 1898 a new type of material was produced called liquid investment which made it much easier to make a mould around a wax model. This meant that small intricate castings could be made quickly and easily with an accuracy previously impossible. Since that time, research into waxes and investment material plus better methods and equipment have brought this branch of metal working, called lost wax investment casting, to a peak of perfection—not only as a creative medium, but also as an essential industrial tool.

Lost wax castings range from life-size statues to fine jewelry and work is cast in gold, silver and platinum as well as base metal.

The method can even be extended by vintage car enthusiasts for making car parts which are no longer stocked.

To the accomplished artist or the beginner, lost wax casting offers a unique extension of his or her creative talent. Designs which would otherwise be impossible to achieve in metal can be made in wax first and a mould can then be made for the metal cast.

This chapter is divided into two sections; a description of the materials used and a general introduction to the techniques of lost wax casting. Subsequent chapters deal with the actual casting of an object.

Basic materials

The basic materials used in this casting process are as follows:

Waxes

Though numerous types of wax are used for lost wax casting, they all have one thing in common and that is that the ash-residue after the burn-out does not exceed 0.1% of the original bulk of wax. If it did, a certain amount of waste wax would remain inside the mould and contaminate the metal.

It must be emphasized that the waxes used are not simple materials. They are mixtures of several ingredients intended to produce a material with definite and reproducible qualities.

The waxes seen in the picture are a

The head of a king, an example of Benin bronze work made using the lost wax method of casting. The Benin of Nigeria still use this method today.

Paul Kemp

combination of animal, vegetable, mineral and synthetic waxes. These are mixed with natural resins such as dammar, kauri or amber and a small percentage of inert fillers such as talc or starch.

The waxes come in a wide array of colours but there is no significance in this except that a darker wax is easier to see if you are carving a model.

Waxes are available as:

Wire wax—offered in round, square, rectangular, half-round sections—generally used for fabricating designs and as sprues.

Sheet wax—preferably transparent for transferring desings.

Carving wax—offered in blocks.

There are a number of proprietary kits which contain selections of these waxes. Ready-made ring shapes are also available. It is worth noting that there is very little difference between the various forms of wax available from different manufacturers; and it is easier to buy by weight.

Investment

This is a blend of materials, which resembles plaster of paris, but includes cristobalite and silicas. It is mixed with water and hardens quickly to give a fine-grained mould material capable of withstanding temperatures of up to 800°C (1500°F).

Special investments withstand even higher temperatures but it is not necessary to consider them for the purpose of casting sterling silver and student's alloy; only metals which have an extremely high melting point require special investment.

The water ratio is always given with each type of investment and must be adhered to. Only the correct consistency in the finished mould will allow the mould gases free passage and prevent pressure cracks.

Metals

Metals which melt at temperatures up to 1000°C (1832°F) can be used depending

An assortment of waxes for lost wax casting. The colour of the wax is not an important consideration when buying.

Melvin Grey

Paul Kemp

The lost wax investment casting technique was used in the manufacture of these professional golfer's irons.

on the desired result. In general, low temperature alloys with large lead and tin content are not used in lost wax casting as they can be cast more easily in other ways.

Metals containing cadmium must be avoided because of the toxic fumes given off during melting. For this reason scrap metals of an unknown origin should be avoided.

Shown here are some of the suitable metals: sterling silver, available as casting grain or casting scrap; student's alloy, a dental practice base metal, which finishes and looks like gold but tarnishes. It is available in small pieces about 19mm ($\frac{3}{4}''$) square by 1mm ($\frac{1}{32}''$) thick. There are also base casting alloys which are generally engineering materials.

Flux
This is necessary to keep the melting metal clean and free from oxides. Its exact nature depends on the metal being melted; for silver and student's alloy, powdered Castaflux can be used or any other borax-based material. Liquid fluxes are not suitable.

Preventing bubbles
Bubbles are the caster's biggest problem. A special liquid on the model helps reduce the formation of surface bubbles on the model while the investment is poured. Several commercial types of 'anti-bubble' liquid are available but a perfectly good solution is made from equal parts of soft green soap and hydrogen peroxide or 1 part washing-up liquid in 3 parts of water.

Technique
The lost wax process follows six basic steps no matter what metal is involved.

The model
A model of the desired object, say a pendant or ring, is made from specially formulated wax. The model may be carved from solid blocks of wax or can be built up from special wax shapes, wires, strips and sheets.

Alternatively, the model itself could be cast by pouring wax into a special flexible mould.

Mounting the model
Models are mounted on to a stand called a sprue base (fig.1). (This stage is sometimes referred to as 'sprueing the model'.) The model is mounted using wires, either wax or metal, which are called sprues. These serve as the 'pour' and 'gates'—through which the molten metal enters the mould. The gates conduct the metal around in the mould and provide a reserve for the contracting metal to draw on. Keep in mind that whatever is wax at this stage will be metal after the casting.

The flow of metal into the mould must be smooth and the passages within the mould along which the metal runs must be arranged so that all parts of the mould are served equally. For lost wax casting using investment, the ways in which the wax model is mounted before being surrounded with investment determines the success of the cast.

Investing
The investment is poured to form the mould. A sprue base is made so that it can be surrounded easily by a metal

Scrap silver and student's alloy with some flux and a mound of investment. The jar contains liquid used to prevent bubbles forming on the wax model.

Melvin Grey

tube called a casting flask (fig.2). Casting flasks can be bought from the suppliers of the casting kits or made from offcuts of metal tubing. Plasticine is used to stop investment seeping out. The sprued model is placed in the flask and the investment material poured around it (fig.3). The investment should be left to set for 30 minutes to complete the initial stiffening. The sprue base is then prised off and any metal sprues removed. This completes the investing and the next step is to remove the wax.

Losing the wax—burn-out

Next the flask is placed upside down in a kiln and heated to about 150°C (325°F) so that the wax model within the investment is melted out—'lost'—leaving a hollow in which the metal is cast. This is the mould (fig.4).

The kiln temperature is then gradually raised to the maximum in order to burn out any wax residue and organic matter, leaving a perfectly clean and dry cavity within the investment. The entire burn-out process takes between 2½-3 hours.

Casting

The chosen molten metal is encouraged to go down the sprues into the mould and take up the shape previously occupied by the wax model and sprue system (fig.5).

Recovery

The rock-hard investment casting is removed by dunking the hot flask into cold water. The sprues and sprue button are sawn off and the object cleaned (fig.6).

The result should be a replica of the original wax model.

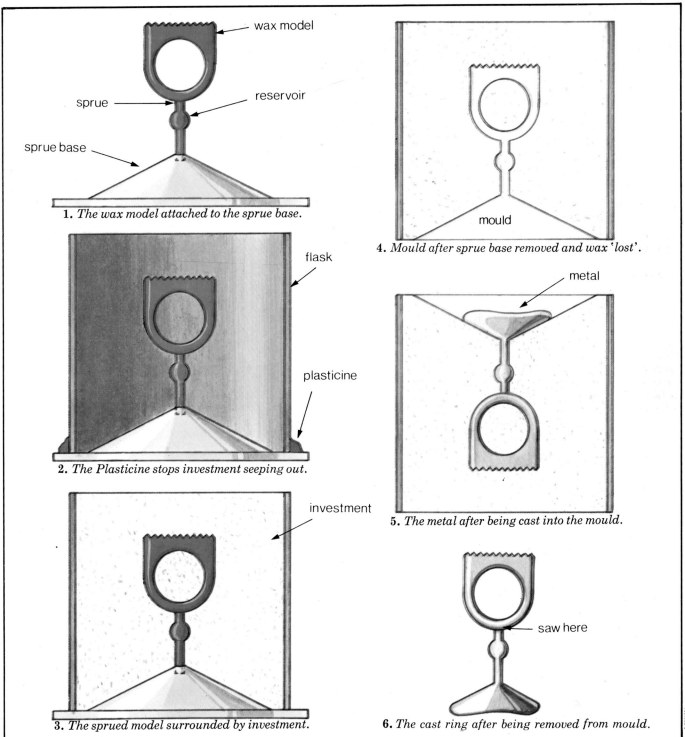

1. *The wax model attached to the sprue base.*

2. *The Plasticine stops investment seeping out.*

3. *The sprued model surrounded by investment.*

4. *Mould after sprue base removed and wax 'lost'.*

5. *The metal after being cast into the mould.*

6. *The cast ring after being removed from mould.*

Paul Williams

1809

An introduction to table looms

The popular table loom may look more complicated than any loom discussed so far but, in fact, the mechanism simplifies and quickens the weaving process while opening up a whole new world of fabric design. The basic weaving principles, of course, remain the same.

As in the roller loom (see Weaving chapter 21, page 1784), the warp of the table loom is stored on rollers to be unwound as needed but extra equipment exists on a table loom to make the process of weaving easier.

Heddles. Instead of the rigid heddle, the table loom has a series of wire or string leashes. These are known individually as heddles or healds. Sets of heddles are attached to movable frames called shafts. The heddles can slide along the shaft and each heddle has an eye through which one warp thread is passed. Each shaft, therefore controls a certain set of warp threads.

The shafts are raised by means of a simple lever system. As the shaft is moved it raises its heddles which in turn pull up the threads, thus forming a shed.

Sheds. When only two sheds are available, as with the roller loom, the basic plain weave structure of under one, over one is the only weave possible. The table loom with more than two shafts can make more than two sheds as shafts can be lifted either on their own or in combinations. On a four-shaft loom, for instance, lifting shafts individually gives four sheds, lifting them in pairs gives six sheds and lifting in threes gives another four sheds. All the sheds will create a completely different effect as different threads are lifted.

The pattern variations available for designing lengths of cloth are therefore endless.

The reed. The other major difference between the table loom with shafts and the simple roller loom is that the table loom has a movable framed comb or reed that spaces and spreads all the warp threads. Each tiny space in the reed is known as a dent. The frame of the reed is known as the batten and it is with this that the cloth is beaten down.

Buying a table loom

When selecting a table loom, you must always bear in mind not only the actual weaving you will want to do but also the space needed to accommodate the equipment.

So decide first on the space available, and then consider what type of loom to buy. This must be thought of very carefully, as you cannot adapt a loom by adding extra shafts and you must

Left: Alison Mitchell, a professional weaver, working on her sixteen-shaft loom.

select the loom to suit your particular aims and aspirations.

Two-way loom: if you are only going to weave small items such as scarves, table mats, shoulder bags etc, this calls for a two-way loom rather like the roller loom shown in Weaving chapter 21, page 1784.

There is one very important point to remember if weaving on a two-way loom. The loom takes some time to thread so if making something short such as the scarf, it is a good idea to put on a long warp for several similar articles at the same time. This saves time as you will only have to thread the loom once.

The two-way loom obviously restricts you to the basic under one, over one of plain weave and for more interesting patterns, a loom with more than two sheds is needed.

The four-shaft loom: the next choice of loom is possibly the most popular loom for home use—a four-shaft table loom. These are available in sizes from 30cm to 80cm (12″ to 32″) weaving widths. Above this width your arms would become very extended and the pleasure of weaving would be lost.

The size of the loom you choose is very much governed by available space but remember that it is not economical to buy a small loom at first and to discover you need a larger one later. The most popular size is 60cm (24″) weaving

width. These looms are capable of weaving tweeds to finish at 55cm (22″) and, of course, all the smaller items already mentioned can be woven. Because you can raise the shafts singly or in any combination you choose, you now have fourteen sheds instead of two. This means that patterns on four shafts are so varied that you could spend a lifetime of home weaving without duplicating a pattern.

If the loom has steel shafts, wire heddles and chains to lift the shafts, carpeting and rugs as well as cloth can be woven to 60cm (24″) width.

There is only one limitation on the 60cm (24″) loom which affects the home weaver. This is that tweeds for men's suitings cannot be produced on it.

If you want to weave for men's clothes, wider fabric will be required—you will need an 80cm (32″) loom.

Of course, a loom of this size becomes a very static piece of equipment taking up a lot of room. However, weaving on a loom this size which has lifting levers in the front central position is quite a joy. It is generally accepted that the larger the loom, the easier it is to operate and the better the work coming off the loom.

Large looms also mean heavy construction which allows one to weave very

Looms come in different widths. This is also a sixteen-shaft model.

Alan Duns

good rugs of carpet wool, either flat kelim rugs or the well-established rya-type pile rug. Even a rug made using unspun wool can be coped with. Small looms cannot accept these rugs round the cloth beam.

Larger looms

So far, only two- and four-shaft looms have been mentioned and these are undoubtedly the most popular with the home weaver. The scope of weaving, however, does not end there.

Eight-shaft looms. For those who

The most popular table loom is the four-shaft model. Here the loom is being used for weaving tapestry.

want to design extensively there are looms with eight shafts in 38cm, 60cm, 70cm and 80cm (15″, 24″, 28″ and 32″) widths.

These looms also have a choice of two warp beams and this allows the weaver to create new ideas using finer yarns and man-made fibres. The second warp beam allows a warp of different tension to be used to make, for instance, a cloth with a looped pile similar to moquette. It also means that you can give cloth the appearance of having a very openly spaced warp directly on top of your basic cloth. Designs are limitless and with these looms you can really have exclusive materials created in your own home.

Sixteen-shaft looms. For more professional designing there is the sixteen-shaft table loom in sizes 38cm and 60cm (15″ and 24″) wide. Industrial designers use them, but so too can the home weaver as more experience is gained. The outlay is not great if you are really going to devote yourself to weaving but this sort of loom is certainly not recommended as a first buy.

Tips when buying

One final word of caution—do choose your loom, whatever the size, with great care. Find out about and look at different types and makes. Never buy direct from an advertisement but visit other weavers, evening classes, manu-

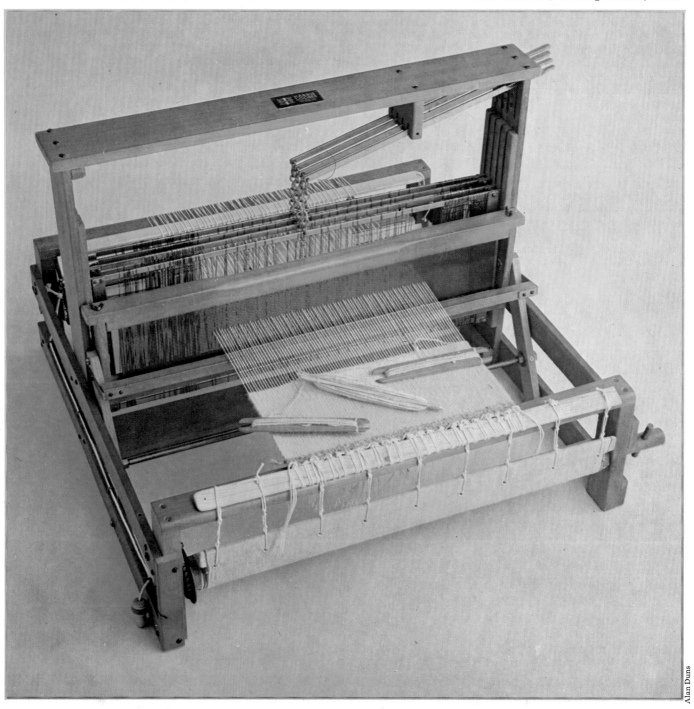

Alan Duns

facturers' showrooms. Ask the loom maker for advice and if you want the loom to operate differently to the stock sample a good company will help you. Finally, buy as large a loom as you can accommodate—it is false economy to start small and to buy bigger looms as you need them. However, first make sure you want to become a weaver before buying any loom.

Table loom terms

Apron. Cloth, usually canvas, with cords attached to the cloth and warp beams.

Batten. Frame of the reed that is used to beat down the fabric being woven.

Castle. Bar structure from which the shafts are suspended.

Cloth beam. Front roller of loom around which the woven cloth is wound. In some books the cloth beam is called the cloth roller.

Dent. A space in the reed. As different reeds are used for different types of fabric, the density of the dents per 2.5cm (1″) in a reed describes the size needed. For example, an eight-dent reed is a reed with eight spaces or dents to 2.5cm (1″). Sometimes, reeds are sold by the number of dents per 10cm (4″), so be careful when buying.

Heddle (heald). Wire or string structure with an eye through which a warp thread is passed. The heddles are attached to the shafts and thus a shed

is formed when the shaft levers are pushed down.

Levers. Table looms have a lever system which pulls up the individual shafts to create the sheds.

Ratchet. Mechanism which holds the beams in place and which allows them to be unrolled. The ratchet also keeps tension on the warp.

Reed. Comb-like structure through which the warp threads are passed. The reed spaces the threads to a particular sett and different-sized reeds are used to create light or heavy fabrics.

Warp beam. Back roller of the loom around which the warp is rolled (see Cloth beam). Some table looms with eight or 16 shafts have two warp beams.

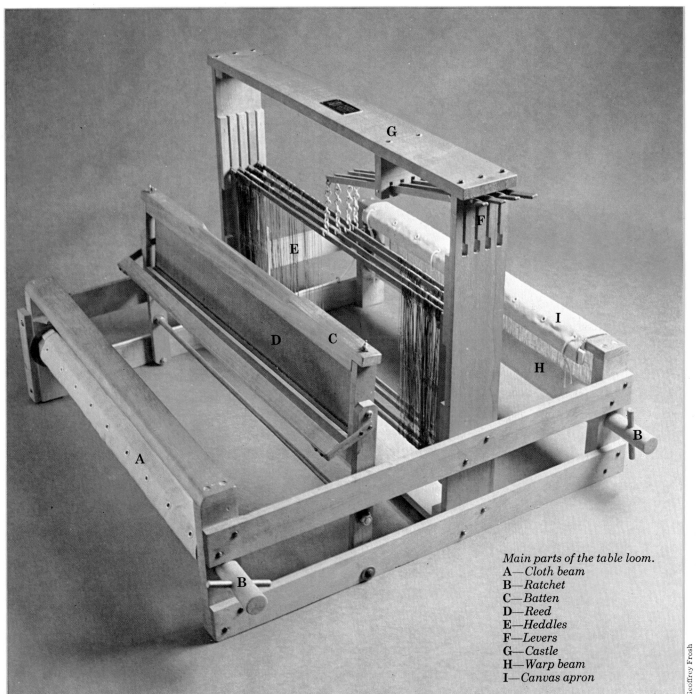

Main parts of the table loom.
A—*Cloth beam*
B—*Ratchet*
C—*Batten*
D—*Reed*
E—*Heddles*
F—*Levers*
G—*Castle*
H—*Warp beam*
I—*Canvas apron*

Geoffrey Frosh

Making a wide-brimmed hat

Cloth — millinery 6

A hat with a wide brim can be very flattering. In Millinery chapter 5, page 1598, a graph pattern and instructions are given for a hat with a stitched brim. Here are instructions on how to adapt that pattern to a hat with a wide stitched brim.

As a useful alternative, instructions are also given for making a brim pattern to any size and shape you wish.

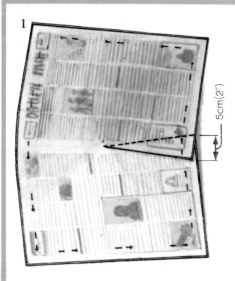

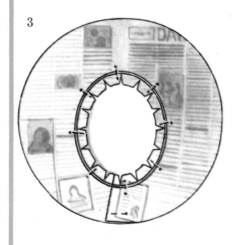

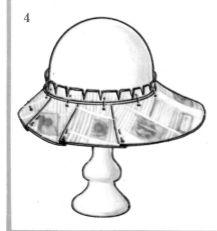

This hat will suit a coquette or a grande dame, depending on how the brim is turned.

Melvin Grey

Making a brim pattern

You will need:

2 large sheets of newspaper.
Headwire made to the correct size.
Steel pins 3cm ($1\frac{3}{16}''$) long.
Paper cutting scissors.
Brown sticky paper (such as Gumstrip).

Two sheets of newspaper are used because one would not be firm enough. Pin sheets together and work as one.

☐ Cut from one edge to the centre. Overlap the cut edges by about 5cm (2") to make a dart and secure with pins to form a shallow cone (fig.1).

☐ Lay the headwire over the point of the cone and pin it in place with at least 8 pins (fig.2).

☐ Measure from the wire down the cone and cut a generous sized brim. Conventionally a downward sloping brim is widest at the sides, narrower at the front and narrowest at the back.

☐ Cut away the paper inside the headwire leaving a 1.5cm ($\frac{5}{8}''$) seam allowance, clip into the turnings every 2cm ($\frac{3}{4}''$)—this will allow the pattern to be tried on the head (fig.3).

Note: this is the only seam allowance on the brim pattern. The centre back and outside edge allowances are added when the fabric and interfacings are cut out.

☐ Place the brim pattern on the block or modelling head so that the slope and style can be adjusted. If the outside edge of the brim is too full, cut through the paper at the points where you wish to reduce the fullness, overlap the cut edges and pin forming darts of up to 1cm ($\frac{1}{4}''$) at the brim edge (fig.4). A number of shallow darts will give a better curve than a few deep ones.

☐ For a turned-up brim the curves in the brim should be well emphasized as they tend to flatten during the making-up process. Replace any pins that fall out with small strips of gummed paper.

☐ The final width of the brim should not be decided until the crown pattern has been pinned on to the brim over the headwire and the proportion checked in a full length mirror, preferably wearing the outfit with which the hat is to be worn.

☐ Before cutting out the brim in fabric and interfacing, cut the pattern through the centre back and add a seam allowance to the back and outside brim edge.

The voile hat

Size: 55cm (22") head.

You will need:

70cm (27") of 90cm (36") wide printed cotton voile.
115cm ($1\frac{1}{4}$yd) of 135cm (54") nylon net.
2 reels of Sylko No.50 in a slightly darker shade than the voile.
70cm ($\frac{3}{4}$yd) millinery petersham ribbon 2cm ($\frac{3}{4}''$) wide.

The brim for this hat is interfaced with four layers of net and made in the same way as the cloche hat (Millinery chapter 5, page 1599). A lining would spoil the transparent effect.

When the hat has been made press it on a block in order to get a good crown shape. If the crown turnings show through, trim them back to the top stitching.

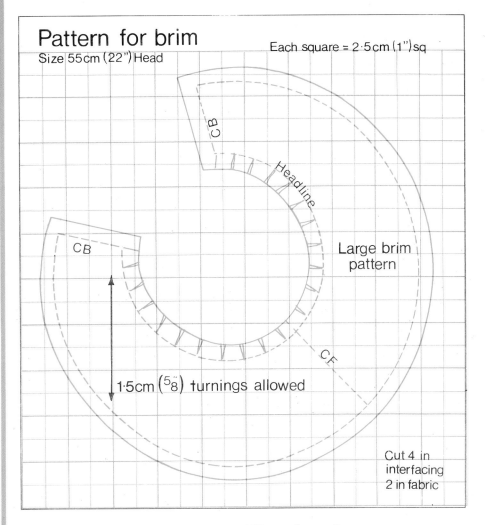

Pattern for brim
Size 55cm (22") Head
Each square = 2·5cm (1") sq

CB
Headline
CB
CF
Large brim pattern
1·5cm ($\frac{5}{8}''$) turnings allowed
Cut 4 in interfacing
2 in fabric

Graph pattern for wide brim to fit hat in Millinery chapter 5.

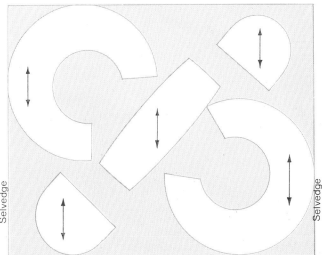

Cutting layout voile hat

Cutting layout includes all pieces required to make the hat.

Selvedge

Selvedge

Trevor Lawrence

How to make a kaleidoscope

The kaleidoscope was invented in the early 19th century and has been popular as a toy ever since. The word 'kaleidoscope' comes from three Greek words: 'kalos' (beautiful), 'edios' (form) and 'skopeo' (look at) and it certainly lives up to its name. Though it is a very simple optical instrument generally using two or three inclined mirrors, it produces an endless number of combinations of symmetrical patterns and designs when bits of coloured glass are moved about and reflected in the mirrors. The kaleidoscope is a source of interest and amusement for adults and children alike, as well as being of value to pattern designers. Perhaps surprisingly, kaleidoscopes are relatively cheap and easy to make. If two mirrors are used they can be inclined at right angles to each other, at a 45° angle or a 60° angle. If three mirrors are used they give a greater number of reflections. They can form an equilateral triangle, or a triangle with angles of 90°, 60° and 30°, or with angles of 90°, 45° and 45°.

The following instructions are for a kaleidoscope with three mirrors forming an equilateral triangle, that is with three angles each of 60°, and 20.5cm (8″) long, since this length is generally considered to produce the best focus. (Light intensity within the kaleidoscope falls off with successive multiple reflections, so that not all the images will be equally bright.)

You will need:
A cardboard tube with an inside diameter of 5cm (2″) and 21cm (8¼″) long. An old poster tube of strong, thick cardboard is suitable.
A piece of thin card, about 26cm x 10cm (10″x 4″).
A piece of acetate or similar film about 6.5cm (2½″) square.
A piece of good quality tracing paper about 6.5cm (2½″) square.
Decorative wrapping paper at least 36cm x 19.5cm (14″x 7¾″).
Three mirrors, each 4.2cm x 20.5cm x 2mm (1⅛″x 8″x 1/16″). It is important that they are precisely cut: you can have this done at a glazier's.
A selection of tiny transparent beads or pieces of flat coloured glass of various shapes and in a wide range of colours.
Adhesive tape.
General-purpose glue.
Pencil, ruler, a pair of compasses.
Scissors or scalpel.
A small hack saw.
□ Using the hack saw, cut the tube into two pieces 20.5cm (8″) and 0.5cm (¼″) long. Cut a piece of wrapping paper 20.5cm x 19.5cm (8″x 7¾″) and cover the longer piece of tube with it. Glue it down (fig.1).

Both adults and children will love the patterns produced by the kaleidoscope.

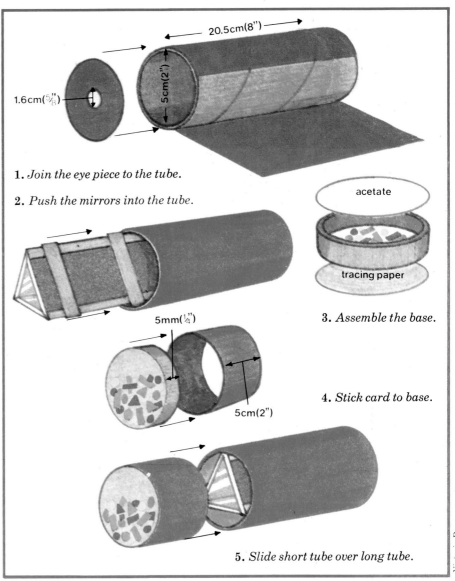

1. *Join the eye piece to the tube.*

2. *Push the mirrors into the tube.*

3. *Assemble the base.*

4. *Stick card to base.*

5. *Slide short tube over long tube.*

Victoria Drew

□ To make the eye piece, place one end of the tube on a piece of thin card and draw round it. Cut out the drawn circle and cover one side of it with wrapping paper. Using the compasses, draw another circle with a diameter of 1.6cm (⅝″) in the centre of the thin card circle and cut it out. Apply glue to one end of the large tube and fix the circle in place (see fig.1).
□ Tape the mirrors together to form an equilateral triangle with all the reflecting sides facing the centre. Push them into the tube (fig.2). They should fit firmly and retain their shape. If they do not fit tightly in the tube, wrap more tape round them at regular intervals until they hold firm.
□ To make the box which will hold the beads or pieces of glass, take the smaller 5mm (¼″) piece of tube and draw round it to make a circle on the tracing paper and one on the acetate. Cut out the circles (fig.3).
□ Carefully apply glue round one edge of this short piece of tube and stick the tracing paper circle to it; this becomes

the base of the kaleidoscope.
□ Now half fill the small tube with an assortment of beads or glass. Use a wide variety of colour and shapes—tiny beads, rod shapes, beads in the shapes of leaves and so on give a marvellous visual effect. You might like to look at the mixture through the longer tube and add or subtract beads until you have the right amount.
□ Then apply glue to the top edge of the tube and fix the acetate in position, enclosing the beads (see fig.3).
□ Take a strip of thin card 19.5cm x 5cm (7¾″x 2″) and cover one side of it with wrapping paper. Bend it round the large tube, overlapping the ends of the card, and glue them together.
□ Separate the newly-formed tube from the original tube, and glue the small tube with the beads into one end of it; the acetate must be inside (fig.4). Slide hollow end over the open end of the long tube (fig.5).
·By looking through the long tube and slowly twisting the end, innumerable patterns will be seen.

Pile trimmings and fabrics

The technique of working a pile surface by needlepoint (Needlepoint chapter 8, page 1776) can also be used on fabric to give an unusual texture for wall hangings, cushions or bags and to make warm bedcovers or simply-shaped garments. The pile may be worked in a design over the whole area of the fabric, or in rows or as a trimming leaving some fabric showing.

The yarn
This can be the same yarn as used for rugs or you could use up scraps of knitting yarn or embroidery wool. You could even mix yarns of different textures for an interesting effect.

The fabric
Canvas and jute backing are the most hard-wearing foundations for floor rugs but for wall hangings, cushions and bags it is possible to work on a hessian foundation which is cheaper and softer than canvas or jute backing and available in a wider range of colours. For garments or bedcovers, the foundation fabric should be wool or linen which will be more comfortable to wear or sleep under than hessian.

In order to insert the pile without distorting the weave of the foundation fabric, weft threads have to be withdrawn in pairs across the width of the fabric so the stitches are worked on the remaining warp threads. For this reason the foundation fabric should be evenly woven with fairly thick threads which are easy to count and withdraw, and which are heavy enough to take the weight of the pile. Furnishing weight hessian and linen and wool fabrics with 16 or 18 threads per 2.5cm (1″) are ideal.

Amount of fabric. Allow the same amount as usual for the item being made.

If you are making a garment, choose a simple pattern with few seams and darts. A waistcoat or poncho is a good choice and either can be effective.

Preparing the fabric
☐ Cut out the fabric allowing the usual amount for turnings. Neaten the raw edges by overcasting or zigzag machine stitch.

☐ Either mark the line of the turnings or the edge of the area on which the pile is to be worked, as appropriate, with tailor's chalk and machine stitch along the line through the single thickness.

☐ Decide on the length of the pile and mark the pairs of threads to be withdrawn, leaving an interval of half the pile length between each pair if you do not wish any background to show between the rows of pile. Leave slightly more than the length of the pile if you do wish the background to show between rows.

Drawing the threads. Carefully cut the threads to be withdrawn 5cm (2″) in from the machined lines at each side. Draw out the threads between the cuts. Using the point of a needle, draw the remaining portions of the threads back to within 5mm ($\frac{1}{4}$″) of the machined

Ghiordes knot is used to make the shaggy surface on this woollen waistcoat and hessian bag.

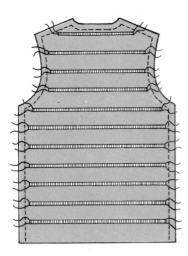

1. *Withdrawing threads to create space for pile stitches. The loose ends are darned in on the wrong side.*

lines (fig.1). Either darn the threads back into the turnings or leave them loose to be darned into the backs of the stitches when the pile has been completed.

Working the pile

The pile is best worked in Ghiordes knot because Surrey stitch tends to distort the fabric. Work the Ghiordes knot as shown in Needlepoint chapter 8, page 1776, treating two fabric threads as half a double bar of canvas and leaving two threads between each stitch (fig.2).

2. *Working the pile stitch.*

Finishing off

Garments and bags. When the pile surface has been completed, make up the item either by machine stitching along the seam line, using a piping foot if necessary, or by back stitching by hand. The wrong side of the fabric will be quite neat but you could add a lining if you wish.

Wall hangings and bedcovers. Fold under the turnings when the pile has been completed, mitre the corners and strengthen the edges by covering with carpet binding (see Latch-hooking chapter 2, page 1132).

Cushions. When the pile has been completed make up the cushion by back stitching or machining the sections together along the seam line.

Woollen fabric is made even warmer by the addition of the colourful pile surface which is stitched on to it.

In this chapter instructions are given for spacing and dividing objects in perspective drawings. There are many occasions when this will be useful such as when drawing a row of books on a shelf, or a line of trees down a street.

Spacing objects. In fig.1 a row of telegraph poles has been drawn along the side of a road. The space between the poles gets smaller as they recede into the distance. The impression given is that the poles are all the same distance apart as they would be in reality. Yet in order to create this impression each one must be drawn progressively closer to the one beside it. It is possible to calculate exactly how far apart each pole should be drawn to convey the impression of equal spacing.

□ Following fig.1, draw the first pole and draw perspective lines from the top and bottom of the pole to the vanishing point (see Design know-how chapter 62, page 1736 for instructions on how to find the vanishing point). The perspective lines determine the height of the other poles which will be drawn smaller as they get further away.

□ Decide the position of the second pole, this can be where you choose, and draw it in. The distance between the first and second poles will determine the distance between the other poles.

□ Draw a line from the centre of the second pole (point A) to the vanishing point. This line will pass through the centre of all poles drawn between the perspective lines.

□ Draw a line (BC) from the bottom of the first pole, through the centre of the second pole, to the top perspective line. Where this line meets the perspective line is the location of the top of the third pole.

□ Draw in the third pole between the perspective lines parallel to the other poles.

□ Draw a line from the bottom of the second pole (point D), through the centre of the third pole to the perspective line (point E). The point where this line intersects the perspective line marks the location for the top of the fourth pole.

□ Continue spacing the poles in this way until either the road ends, or the vanishing point is reached.

This method of spacing can be used successfully to draw any number of similar objects in a given space.

Dividing shapes. When you want to draw an object a certain number of times in a space, or divide a shape into a specific number of sections a different method of spacing is used. In fig.2, a window with four vertical panes has been drawn. The drawn width of each pane is different depending on how far away it is, yet the impression conveyed —as with the poles—is that the panes are all the same size.

□ First draw the outline of the window in perspective. Mark the vanishing point by extending top and bottom lines.

□ Divide the left hand side of the window into four equal horizontal sections—if you want to draw a window with five panes divide the left-hand side of the window into five sections.

□ Draw lines from points A, B and C to the vanishing point.

□ Draw a diagonal line across the window.

Where the diagonal line crosses the lines from A, B and C marks the location for the three uprights dividing the four panes.

□ Draw the uprights parallel to the sides of the window.

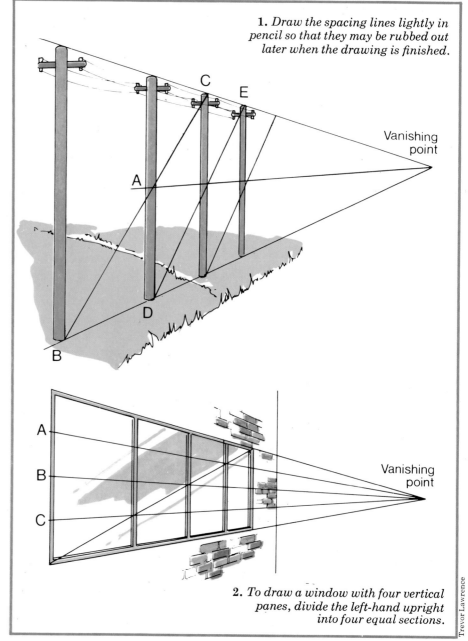

1. *Draw the spacing lines lightly in pencil so that they may be rubbed out later when the drawing is finished.*

2. *To draw a window with four vertical panes, divide the left-hand upright into four equal sections.*

Trevor Lawrence

Creative ideas 65

Hoop-la game

Along with hide-and-seek, this game is a children's favourite and a good idea to have at parties. This particular hoop-la stands up in the soil outdoors, or in a plant pot indoors.

(The cut-out hoop centres fit together on to the dowel rod for the base.)

You will need:

37cm ($14\frac{1}{2}"$) square of plywood 3mm ($\frac{1}{8}"$) thick.

34.2cm ($13\frac{1}{2}"$) of dowelling 19mm ($\frac{3}{4}"$) in diameter.

Coping saw.

Drill or brace with bits for drilling a 3mm ($\frac{1}{8}"$) and a 19mm ($\frac{3}{4}"$) hole.

Wood primer, undercoat and gloss paints.

Medium-grade glasspaper or similar sandpaper.

Woodworking adhesive and wood filler.

Surform or rasp file.

Pair of compasses, pencil and ruler, paintbrush.

Using compasses and pencil, draw four circles on the plywood, each with a 9cm ($3\frac{1}{2}"$) radius. Cut out with coping saw. (See Carpentry chapter 8, page 548.)

To make the hoop-la base draw a smaller concentric circle in each of these, with a 6cm ($2\frac{1}{4}"$) radius (see fig. 1a).

Drill a 3mm ($\frac{1}{8}"$) hole just inside the circumference of each inner circle. Insert the coping saw blade through this hole and secure to handle. Cut out inner circle from this point. The four outside circles make the hoops to throw at the base. Glue inner circles together to make base and fill the drill holes with wood filler. Using 19mm ($\frac{3}{4}"$) bit, drill a hole through base (fig.1b). With a Surform tool or rasp file, shape one end of the dowel to a point. Apply glue 11cm ($4\frac{1}{4}"$) from point. Insert through base (fig.1c).

Smooth each of the rings and base with glasspaper. Prepare hoop-la with primer and undercoat. Finish with gloss paints.

Designer: Roger Polley.

Good judgement and a skilful flick of the wrist ensure a winning throw.

Sandra Lousada

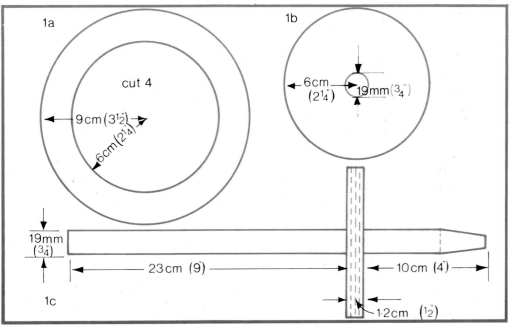

1a — cut 4 — 9cm ($3\frac{1}{2}"$) — 6cm ($2\frac{1}{4}"$)

1b — 6cm ($2\frac{1}{4}"$) — 19mm ($\frac{3}{4}"$)

1c — 19mm ($\frac{3}{4}"$) — 23cm (9") — 10cm (4") — 1·2cm ($\frac{1}{2}"$)

Trevor Lawrence

Mounting prints and pictures

Mounting photographs, prints, pictures or any two-dimensional item serves a number of purposes, both practical and aesthetic. Putting prints between two good-quality mounting boards (one of which acts as a backing board and one of which is a 'window' framing the print) will prevent them from becoming damaged and will preserve them in good condition for many years. Even a picture or photograph of mediocre quality will be greatly improved when mounted, and small defects such as a crease or fold will become far less noticeable.

A picture which is attractive unmounted will become emphatically so when mounted; the space created round it by the mount enables it to be seen better, since it has been separated from the background and given importance. For all these reasons, it is well worth spending a small amount of money and perhaps an hour of your time to enhance a favourite picture.

There are no strict rules concerning mounting, only a number of guidelines. One of these is that it is usual to mount a picture centrally as regards width, but with a slightly bigger border at the lower edge. This balances the composition visually and is especially desirable for prints which have a caption beneath.

Proportions

When choosing proportions for picture and mount, first consider whether the picture is vertical or horizontal. Generally speaking, the mount should be of a similar shape to the image, regardless of the actual width of the border. The more you want to isolate a picture from its surroundings and make it stand out, the larger the border should be. You may decide that your picture—especially if it is a photograph —needs trimming in order to emphasize the subject matter, and this must be taken into consideration when you decide on the size of the mount.

The colour of the mount will also affect the visual size of the picture within it: a light colour will make the picture seem smaller than if it were enclosed by a dark border. These are the reasons for choosing between large and small, and light and dark borders, but all may be used out of context in order to create a striking, interesting or unusual effect. The final decision depends entirely on your personal taste.

Colour and texture

Choice of materials is also largely a matter of individual taste and depends on the picture you are mounting. The

Neil Lorimer

The individuality of a print or photograph is heightened by the shape of the border, in this case an archway.

mounting card must of course be heavy enough to support the picture and prevent warping. Bear in mind that the idea of mounting is to display the picture, and therefore the border should compliment it by being in keeping with the mood depicted. A mounting board in a softer version of the predominant colour of the picture is often successful. Strong or brilliant colours should be used with care, since they may detract from the picture displayed.

If you are mounting directly on to textured board, make sure that the texture will not come through and damage the print. If you fear this may happen, first mount the print on light card and then mount this on to the textured board.

Special card known as mounting board is suitable for the majority of purposes, and can be bevelled quite easily to give a neat finishing touch.

Other materials, such as wood, aluminium or even plastic, can also be used and can have attractive results.

A simple mount

The following example is given as a guide to the method of simple window mounting which you can adapt to suit your own pictures. The diagram (fig.1)

1

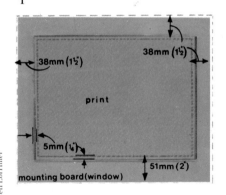

1. *Size of border round the print.*

Fine black border lines drawn round the mount with felt-tipped pen can help to emphasize a picture.

shows a print around which it has been decided to put a 38mm (1½″) border along the top and sides and a 51mm (2″) border at the bottom.

All prints will lose 5mm (¼″) all round when they are placed beneath the mount window, so that their effective size is smaller than their actual size.

You will need:

Mounting board of twice the size of the finished mount.

Picture to be mounted.

Rubber-based adhesive such as Cow Gum and spatula.

Craft knife or scalpel.

Metal ruler, pencil, felt-tipped pen (optional).

☐ Cut two identical pieces of mounting board the size of the print plus 66mm (2½″) in width and 79mm (3″) in length. One of these becomes the backing board for the mount and the other the window.

☐ On the back of the window piece,

These three examples show the different effects produced by a dark, light and

brightly coloured border round the same print. Consider the colour of the wall

against which it is being hung, when choosing the mount.

where pencil marks will not show, divide the board into four equal parts (fig.2).

☐ On the horizontal axis measure half the width of the print minus 5mm ($\frac{1}{4}$") each side of the centre and draw two vertical parallel lines (see fig.2).

☐ On the vertical axis measure half the height of the print above the centre and half the height of the print minus 10mm ($\frac{1}{2}$") below, and draw two horizontal parallel lines. This then gives a rectangle the size of the print minus 5mm ($\frac{1}{4}$") all round.

☐ Carefully cut out this rectangle (see fig.2) with a craft knife and metal ruler. (See bevel cutting, below.)

☐ Take the second piece of board (the backing board) and find its centre by dividing the board into four equal parts (fig.3).

☐ Measure the outside of the print so that it can be accurately located on the backing board.

☐ Measure half the width of the print on each side of the vertical axis and draw two parallel lines, and half the height of print plus 5mm ($\frac{1}{4}$") above horizontal axis and half the height of the print minus 5mm ($\frac{1}{4}$") below to give a rectangle the size of the whole print (see fig.3).

☐ Glue the print in position with Cow Gum, squeezing out all air bubbles, and allow to dry before cleaning off any excess gum.

☐ Glue the window board on the base-

To draw a line or lines round a mount, use a metal ruler and felt-tipped pen.

board with the print sandwiched between the two, taking great care not to allow any glue to adhere to the print. (For assembly, see fig.4.)

☐ A fine felt-tipped pen line may be drawn round the edge of the print for decoration, if desired.

This simple method of mounting can be adapted to solve most problems posed by picture display, once the basic decisions of border, width and colour have been made.

Bevel cutting

Bevel cutting is a variation on the simple straight line cut with a knife. Here the blade is tilted at about a 45° angle against the inner edge of the window board (which has already been drawn) and an angled cut or edge results. This will work only on straight line cuts unless a template is made to the particular shape desired. It is advisable to practise on scraps before attempting to cut the actual mount.

Unusual shapes

Apart from straight-edged windows there are many other shapes which may be used as mounting windows.

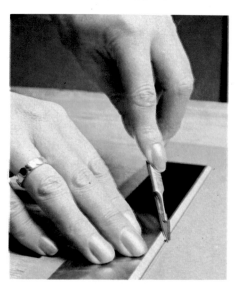

When bevel cutting the blade should rest against a ruler at a 45° angle.

The oval has always been popular for mounting miniatures and portraits. Archways, hexagons, circles and even asymmetrical shapes can be used to advantage in many cases. Fig.5 indicates an archway formed by a semi-circle placed on a square or rectangle, while fig.6 shows a fairly simple method of drawing an oval by constructing two adjacent circles and then joining them with the help of a pair of compasses. You can use a template made of thin card if you are cutting curved lines.

Figs.7 and 8 show a simple method of making a three-dimensional mount. Glue the print to a piece of thick card and measure a narrow, even border all around it (fig.7). Then measure a

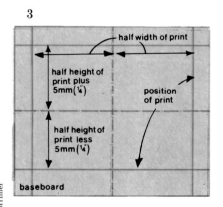

2. *Measuring the window piece.*
3. *Positioning print on baseboard.*
4. *Method of assembly.*

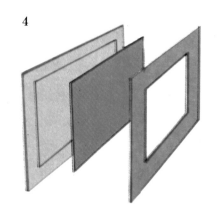

Neil Lorrimer

Left: an unusual circular mount reflects the shape of the picture itself.

Above: a simple oval mount is the classical way of mounting portraits, whether traditional or modern.

further border around the first one, to the depth you wish the box to be. Cut out the card as shown and score it with a sharp knife along the dotted lines (see fig.7). Bend back the edges and glue them together (see fig.8).

No doubt you will be able to devise many other shapes and methods of construction to display your own prints and pictures. The important thing to remember is that, throughout every stage of mounting, care, precision and cleanliness are of the utmost importance.

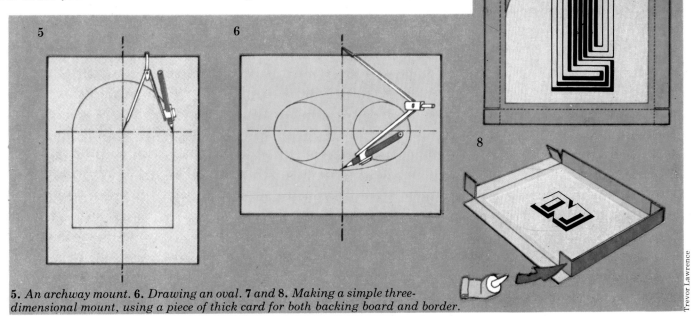

5. *An archway mount.* **6.** *Drawing an oval.* **7** *and* **8.** *Making a simple three-dimensional mount, using a piece of thick card for both backing board and border.*

Trevor Lawrence

Decorative tile making

Tile making is one of the simplest activities in pottery—but the results do not have to be simple, they can be complex, unusual, dramatic and exciting.

Any decorative technique open to the potter can be applied to tiles—they can be smooth or textured, they can be any shape—flat or curved, in relief or pierced through, glazed or unglazed. Because of all these possibilities it is not necessary to think of them solely in terms of their traditional uses as floor, wall and table coverings. The tiles illustrated here were all designed as decorative panels, to lie on a surface, to be hung like a picture or to be free-standing, like a sculpture.

Clay

All clay shrinks as it dries and, unless it is made into a stable structure, it can easily distort at the same time. Flat slabs of clay, such as tiles, are particularly susceptible to this kind of distortion unless the body is specially prepared to counteract the problem. For this reason ordinary clay is seldom suitable for tiles—except for very small ones. Ready-mixed tile clay can be purchased from pottery suppliers, but it is quite easy to prepare your own by adding approximately 25% fine grog to ordinary clay.

Slice the clay thinly. Add a little water to a fine grog and use it as a filling between the slices. Then knead and wedge the clay very thoroughly to disperse the powder evenly.

The same batch of clay should be used for all the tiles in a panel, and working conditions should be fairly constant throughout their manufacture. This is, of course, particularly important when creating intricate interlocking designs. **Testing for shrinkage.** Even when the correct clay is used, there will still be a certain amount of shrinkage, which must be taken into account when designing a covering for a surface area of a particular size. It is as well to carry out a simple test to check the performance of the clay through drying and firing.

Cut small sample tiles of precise dimensions from a piece of rolled clay of known thickness. Allow the tiles to dry, fire them up to glazing temperature and then measure them again. Use the two sets of measurements to calculate the fraction of shrinkage. You can use the information thus obtained to calculate the number of tiles needed for the panel.

1. *Inset, shows the almost wood-like effect of stencilling with oxides. All tiles designed by Tony Jolly.*
2. *The background shows the textured surfaces created by impressing found objects into damp clay.*

Basic tile making

The basic materials remain the same for all kinds of tiles, as do the methods of cutting and working. Instructions here are for a batch of 6 to 8 tiles, each 10cm (4″) square.

You will need:

About 1kg (2lb) prepared clay.

Thick ply or chipboard, about 75cm x 50cm (30″ x 20″), as a cutting/drying surface.

Rolling pin, wooden laths.

Sharp knife or commercial tile cutter.

Old ceramic tiles for weighting drying tiles.

Thick card template, cut to dimensions required.

Modelling tools, ruler.

Small board for flattening tiles.

Light polythene cover, Surform files.

Fine glasspaper and wire wool.

Because handling should be kept to a minimum, it is wise to roll out and cut the clay directly on the drying board—a piece of ply or chipboard is an ideal drying board and working surface.

Clay can be cut with a knife using a template, or with a commercial tile cutter which works on the same principle as a pastry cutter. Different tile cutters produce different sizes and shapes of tile.

☐ Roll out a sheet of clay, on the board, using wooden laths to ensure an even overall thickness of about 5mm (¼″). Smaller tiles should be fractionally thinner, larger tiles fractionally thicker.

☐ Turn the clay over from time to time during the rolling process to check that the reverse side is smooth and to ensure that the sheet of clay does not adhere to the working surface.

☐ Use the point of the knife and the ruler to mark out the tiles. Check that the dimensions are correct before cutting.

If you are using a tile cutter, it is not necessary to mark the lines before cutting.

☐ Cut the tiles with firm, steady movements, using the marks and the ruler itself as a guide.

☐ Remove the scrap clay for further use and allow the tiles to dry out slightly.

☐ Check for signs of warping and, if you find any, turn the affected tiles over and gently flatten them out with the small board.

☐ Once these basic tiles can be handled without distortion, stack them in piles of 8 to 10 under an old ceramic tile and leave them until they are leather-hard. If, however, you have designed tiles with irregular surfaces, they must be spread out to dry, not stacked, with small gaps between them to allow air to circulate. Cover them with polythene, but remove it from time to time to speed up the drying-out.

3. Wooden type suggests a design.

☐ When the tiles are leather-hard, use the card template to check the shape of each one, and also examine them for surface irregularity.

☐ Use Surform files and modelling tools to remove any variations.

☐ Lightly press the tiles between the small board and the working surface before re-stacking them to complete the drying process.

☐ When dry, finish off both surfaces of each tile with glasspaper (or wire wool if the tiles are particularly small or intricate in form).

☐ Use the glasspaper to round off the edges very slightly and to bevel the corners.

Keep the tiles as dust-free as possible until you are ready to glaze them. Brush down all surfaces, to remove clay dust, before applying glaze.

Glazing flat tiles. Tiles should be grasped at the edges between thumb and fingertips, held upside down and dipped into the raw glaze.

Make sure that the glaze is stirred frequently and that each tile is immersed for exactly the same length of time to ensure a common glaze thickness. In each case, after applying glaze, clean the back of the tile thoroughly with a damp sponge.

Firing

If two or more firings are required to complete a large batch of tiles, the packing scheme for successive firings should be as similar as possible. The rate of temperature rise, also, should be the same for each firing.

Most tiles can be laid directly on the kiln shelves, but larger panels, which have to rest on uneven or divided shelves, should be bedded in a layer of silver sand for support.

Decorative tiles

Several examples of tile decoration are given here, all of which can be applied to basic tiles.

Stencilled tiles. The fifteen stencilled tiles in the inset on opposite page, each 9cm (3½″) square (see fig.1) were cut out with a commercial tile cutter.

Paper stencils were designed and cut out with sharp scissors. Paper which had been folded during the cutting was ironed before use.

The decoration was applied to biscuit tiles, using a sponge to stipple a mixture of red iron oxide, manganese oxide and underglaze medium through the stencil.

After stencilling, the tiles were raw glazed with a mottled tan glaze containing a small proportion of manganese oxide, and then fired in the usual way. Fairly complex designs can be applied using this technique, but remember that, as the pigment has to bleed through the glaze, the outline of the design will not be crisp.

Press-patterned tiles in background panel opposite. This panel (fig.2), is prepared with the same commercial tile cutter as before. Each has a low surface relief pattern applied with the fingers themselves or with a hand-held object. Press-patterns should be applied before the tiles are cut.

Mark out the area of each tile with knife and rule, or with tile cutter. Complete the press decoration within each marked area before cutting the tiles free of the sheet of clay.

A wide variety of found objects can be used to achieve this kind of effect. Those used in this case were wooden modelling tools, keys, ruler ends, pieces of scrap from a plastic modelling kit, nuts and bolts, metal and wood offcuts, animal teeth, sea shells, fir cones, pieces of broken kiln element and bottle tops.

The glaze on these tiles contains a small percentage each of cobalt carbonate and manganese oxide which together produce a muted blue.

When glazing pressed or textured tiles, dip them in the usual way but move them gently up and down to work the glaze into the depressions.

Large single panel. Tiles need not be rectangular or even regular in outline. The large panel (fig.3) was impressed with wooden printing type. It was cut

out in one piece so that the outline followed the edge of the patterned area. Two hanging holes were drilled before the panel was fired. Manganese and copper oxides were rubbed dry into the surface of the biscuit-fired piece before raw glazing.

Circular tiles. Any hollow form can be used as a tile cutter provided the rim is thin and therefore unlikely to distort the clay as it is pressed through. The circular tiles in this hanging (fig.4) were made with the help of an empty food can and the cap of a lipstick.

The clay was rolled out to about 8mm ($\frac{1}{3}$″) and the rim of the food can used to mark the outline of each tile. The large holes within each tile were then cut away with the lipstick cap. The can was then used again to cut each tile free of the clay.

When the tiles had dried to the leather-hard stage, they were drilled with a small-diameter metalworking drill bit. Each hole was chamfered from both sides with a wire loop modelling tool.

A wood-ash glaze was used which gave the variation in surface colour between brown and a pale greenish tan.

The finished tiles were tied together with linen thread and suspended from a hardwood batten.

Glass-inlaid tiles. Any kind of coloured glass can be used to achieve this effect (fig.5) so long as the colour goes all through the glass and is not simply a surface stain. The glass—in this case bottle glass—should be closely wrapped in thick fabric and smashed with a hammer. If you try this, be very wary of splinters, and always work well away from clay or clay working areas. Fine particles of broken glass are almost impossible to see but can

5. *Below: coloured glass melted into depressions in the clay adds another dimension to patterned tiles.*

6. *Relief decoration applied to plain tiles. Any forms can be used, so long as they are in proportion.*

cause nasty cuts—particularly if encountered when working with clay on the wheel.

These tiles were cut from a sheet of clay some 2cm ($\frac{3}{4}''$) thick. The surface of each was cut and patterned with a knife and modelling tools. They were biscuit fired and then raw glazed in white and sponge stippled with copper oxide. The depressions were then part-filled with broken glass before the final firing. It is important not to overfill the depressions because glass is very fluid at high glazing temperatures and should not be allowed to overflow on to the kiln shelf.

Relief tile. Each tile in the small group (fig.6) carries a relief decoration formed by pieces of clay fixed to a flat base, leaving a plain border some 1.25cm ($\frac{1}{2}''$) wide.

The component parts of tiles such as this can be joined together when quite soft or when leather-hard—but each piece should be at the same stage. Pieces of soft and leather-hard clay should never be joined together because they invariably distort or split apart due to unbalanced shrinkage during drying.

When joining clay pieces, ensure that both faces of a join are scored and covered with slip before they are pressed together. Any excess slip which squeezes out from the joint can be removed with a modelling tool. These tiles must be dried on a flat surface under a covering of light polythene and the glaze should be poured over them, because the usual dipping method will not be adequate.

Fixing tiles

The adhesive required will depend upon the surface to which the tiles are to be attached. Builder's merchants supply a cement suitable for wall mounting, and hardware shops offer a range of glues capable of attaching ceramic to a

range of other materials. Consider the nature of the materials to be joined, the quantity of adhesive needed, and the likely cost of all alternatives before making a purchase.

If tiles are to be fixed to a wall or floor, or mounted to form a plaque, the joints between them may have to be filled with a grouting medium. This should be used in accordance with the manu-facturer's instructions. Tiles should be left ungrouted for at least twenty-four hours after fixing. Grout is generally white but it can be tinted by the addition of pigments, such as powdered tempera colour.

These illustrations show just a few of the possibilities in decorative tile making. Further techniques are discussed in a later chapter.

Tony Jolly

Re-covering a modern armchair

Graham Henderson

This chapter describes how to re-cover modern armchairs and settees and how to replace the upholstery if they were originally padded with foam. Details on how to replace traditional upholstery (with springs and horsehair) are given in a later chapter. Alternatively you can replace traditional upholstery with foam as described here.

Foam upholstery

The major change in upholstery over the last decade is the increasing use of foam rubber for the padding instead of 'loose' fillings like horsehair and fibre. Foam is both cheaper and easier to use than a loose filling but it does not last as long and, with regular use, tends to lose its resilience and depth after a few years. Therefore, when the cover fabric needs replacing on chairs upholstered with foam it makes sense to replace the upholstery at the same time. If your furniture was upholstered by traditional methods it probably does not need more than the wadding replaced, so you can simply follow the instructions for replacing the cover.

sketches as you work of how each layer is attached to the frame.

The cover. Remove the bottoming (the piece of fabric on the underside of the chair) and the cover fabric (beginning with the outside back and arms), following the method in Upholstery chapter 8, page 1706. Make a careful note of any edges which were slip-stitched and back-tacked (for description of these processes see Upholstery chapter 5, page 748).

Flies. When you remove the cover you may find that strips of hessian or calico have been stitched on to some of the edges. These are known as flies and are a technique used by some manufacturers as a means of saving cover fabric in places where it is not seen on the chair—on the seat at the sides and back cover or on the inside back below arm level and along the bottom. Do not unpick these sections when estimating the amount of new fabric required but treat the section as a whole—there is no need to make flies on the new cover because the saving in fabric for one individual chair is small. Unpick any other sections of the cover which are seamed and iron out all the pieces so that they can be used as a template for the new cover.

Remove any calico lining covering the foam and discard it.

The foam. If the chair has foam padding examine it before removing it from the frame in case any of it can be reused. Seat cushion foam will almost certainly have suffered compression set (reduction in thickness) as will the foam on top of the arms, and this should be replaced. Generally the padding on the inside back of the chair and the inside arms remains in quite good condition and needs to be removed only if very thin and crumbling, or if the webbing or canvas beneath these pieces needs attention.

The springing. Most armchairs upholstered in foam have either tension springs or rubber webbing beneath the foam and this should be replaced if broken or flabby, following the method described in Upholstery chapter 8.

On some chairs, however, the seats may have a spring unit—a set of coil springs joined by metal strips. Examine this carefully to see if it is broken in any way. If, for example, one of the clips connecting the springs to the metal strips has broken it can be replaced with a piece of wire. If the hole into which the clip is inserted has worn through, you can drill another hole and place the clip in that. If one of the springs has actually broken, it is usually possible to replace it with a coil spring of a similar size.

Unfortunately, if the whole unit is badly damaged or rusty it is not usually possible to replace it with a new unit of

Of course there are many different styles of easy chair but the methods of construction are very similar and many of the basic principles are similar to those already covered in earlier upholstery chapters.

However, many of the details are different and it is helpful to make notes as you strip off the old upholstery.

Two popular styles of armchair, padded with foam and with rubber webbing below the loose seat cushion. The same techniques are used for settees.

Stripping old upholstery

Do this before you buy any new materials so that you can see exactly what you will need. Make notes and the correct size because the old one would have been made for that specific chair. In this case, the whole unit should be discarded and substituted with rubber webbing and new rails to which it can be attached.

New rails. Make these from softwood measuring 50mm x 25mm (2″x 1″) by the inside measurement of the section of the seat frame to which they are to be attached.

Using a 3mm (⅛″) drill bit, drill holes through 50mm (2″) face of the softwood at the centre and 2.5cm (1″) from the ends of both pieces. Screw the rails in position on the frame so they will be level with the base of the seat cushion. The new webbing can be tacked to the tops of the rails.

Jute webbing. On some chairs the foam on the arms and back is supported by jute webbing which should be replaced if torn, following the method in Upholstery chapter 9, page 1732. Hessian over the webbing and on the front border should also be replaced.

Checking the frame
Before starting the new upholstery, check the frame carefully and make any repairs necessary as described in the previous upholstery chapter.

The new materials
Foam. When replacing foam buy the best quality foam you can afford in the correct density—that is, the load-bearing quality. Take the measurements from the chair frame for each

piece of foam that needs replacing, making a paper template for any curved or shaped pieces. Allow 5mm (¼″) all round each piece where you will be forming square edges and 2.5cm (1″) all round for rounded edges.

Density. This is a term used to describe the load-bearing qualities of polyether (synthetic) foam which is most commonly used in upholstery. The density does not affect the feel of the foam which can be chosen to suit your own preference.

High-density foam such as 27kg-30.5kg per cu metre (1.5lb-1.8lb per cu ft) should be used for the area of the chair which takes most pressure, such as the seat and tops of arms. A lower density of 21kg-28kg per cu metre (1 lb to 1.5lb per cu ft) can be used for backs and inside arms.

To judge the thickness of the foam required, measure the corresponding piece of old foam and round up the measurement to the nearest thickness available. If you are in doubt, as a general guide firm seating cushions should be about 7.5cm (3″) thick and soft seat cushions 10cm (4″) thick. Back padding should be about 5cm (2″) thick. The padding for arms, however, varies from 2.5cm (1″) to 4cm (1½″) according to the design of the chair.

Cover fabric. Like the foam, this should be the best you can afford and must be of a correct upholstery grade which will give good wear and can be cleaned easily. If you specifically want a fabric which is not really an uphol-

stery grade, such as some linen unions, it would be more sensible to tight-cover the chair with calico and make the main cover loose so that it can be easily removed for cleaning and repair. If you do decide to make a calico cover, you do not need to line the foam with calico as described below.

To calculate the amount of cover fabric required for a tight cover, lay out the unpicked pieces of the old cover on the floor with the lengthwise grain running the same way on each piece.

Arrange the pieces with about 7.5cm (3″) to spare all round each one so they make up approximately the width of the fabric—usually 120cm-128cm (48″-50″) wide.

Measure the length of the laid-out pieces and add about 45cm (18″) if you are using patterned fabric and another 45cm (18″) if you intend to pipe the cover.

Calico. Although this may not have been done on the original, the parts of the chair which are padded with foam should always be covered with calico to help protect the foam and to give a better surface for the cover fabric. To calculate how much calico you need, lay out the pieces of cover which went over the original foam to make up the available width of calico, which can be anything from 90cm-180cm (36″- 72″), and measure the length as for the main cover. You will also need calico strips for attaching the foam. Allow enough to cut 10cm (4″) wide strips to fit the perimeter of each foam section.

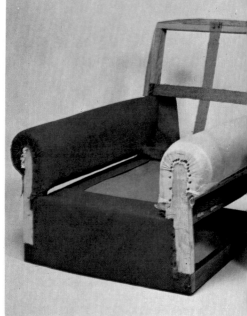

1. *For scroll arms (the chair on the left) the webbing is attached horizontally to give a firm foundation for the hessian. To form the correct shape, this is tacked to the arm tack bar, smoothed over the* arm *and then tacked just below the scroll on outside. On cap-armed chairs (right) webbing is tacked in vertical strands and the hessian is placed on the inside arm over it.*

2. *For scroll arms the rounded shape is formed by attaching the padding and then the cover fabric in a piece which follows the line of the hessian. The fronts of the arms are covered by*

Piping cord. Piping the edges or seams of the cover adds to the tailored appearance of the chair and it is essential if you are using patterned fabric which is usually impossible to match where the panels of the cover meet.

If the old cover was piped, you can calculate the amount of new piping required by measuring the amount used before. If you are adding piping, measure the edges where you intend to place it and add extra for fitting.

If you intend to loose-cover the chair, the calico cover should not be piped.

The new upholstery

Start by cutting out the cover fabric and calico lining, using the old pieces of cover as patterns. Add 7.5cm (3") all round each piece to allow for easy fitting. From the remaining cover fabric cut bias strips for the piping casing. From the remaining calico cut the 10cm (4") wide strips for edging the foam.

Preparing the foam. Glue the calico strips to the foam, placing them along the side face if you want square edges or along the front face if you want rounded edges (the previous upholstery chapter shows both these processes).

Attaching the new upholstery. After any springing has been added it is usually easiest to complete the padding and covering in each section before beginning the next section. Start with the arms, then do the back and finally the seat, applying the padding and cover following the pattern of the original upholstery. If you have a loose

seat cushion with no padding below it, cover the front border after the arms. Where you have sections of fabric which are stitched together before they are attached to the frame, fit the pieces on the chair and pin them together as for a loose cover (see Sewing chapter 18, page 1552). Machine stitch the sections together, with piping in the seams of the top cover. If your seat has a loose cushion, make up the cover for this, following the method in Sewing chapter 7, page 430.

Platforms. On seats with loose seat cushions, the rubber webbing can be finished with a simple fabric cover called a platform. To prevent this fabric from tearing when the webbing expands during use, it is tacked to the frame along the front edge only and strips of elastic are attached to the back edge so it can be tied to the back seat rail. The loose side edges are hemmed and covered by strips of cover fabric which are tacked to the front, back and side edges. (These strips give a finished appearance when the cushion is put on the seat.)

The front border can then be back-tacked along the front edge of the frame, taken under the front strand of webbing and then tacked in place.

Lining capped arms. When lining capped arms which will be tight-covered by fabric, cut the calico to cover the inside and top of the arm only. Tack the edge of the calico to the arm tack bar, smooth it up over the foam and tack the other edge to the

outside arm frame. The side edges of the calico can be tacked to the inside faces of the arms or left loose.

Styles of arm

The arms of most easy chairs are of the styles known as scroll (fig.1, left) or capped (fig.1, right).

For scroll arms the fabric covering the inside arm is tacked to the frame along the tack rail and then pulled tightly over the padding on the top of the arm. It is tacked to the outside arm at the top and to the scroll on the front of the arms, where it is often pleated. The front of the arm is covered with a separate piece of fabric which may either be slip-stitched in position or attached by a separate wood facing which is screwed on to the scroll. Piping is often inserted into the join and may either be tacked to the frame or stitched to the seam line of the fabric. The outside arm is covered by a separate piece of fabric which is usually back-tacked along the top edge, slip-stitched along the side edges and tacked to underside along bottom edge.

For capped arms, the pieces of fabric for the inside and outside sections are stitched to a strip which covers the top and front of the arms before being attached to the chair frame. The seams are often piped. The bottom edges of the fabric are tacked to the frame and, on the outside back and front, covered by the edges of the adjoining panels which are slip-stitched in position. These joins may be piped (see fig.3).

Paul Kemp

separate pieces of fabric which are cut to shape and slip-stitched in position. On cap arms the square shape is made by using the foam in two pieces and making the cover with a piped welt.

3. The backs and seats of both chairs are padded and covered in the same way. Notice how the hessian is left loose below the webbing until the cover fabric has been pulled through and tacked to

the frame. The seats are spanned with rubber webbing and covered with a fabric platform; the top edge of the front border was back-tacked to the frame and pulled over the webbing.

Water gilding

The final result; the gilded frame has been burnished and then distressed.

Paul Kemp

Water gilding is the aristocrat of gilding techniques and is used for really fine interior work. It is an ancient art dating back at least to the 13th century.

This method has several advantages over oil gilding. Its main advantage is its versatility: with oil gilding the finish is a uniformly matt one whereas with water gilding various finishes are possible. Because the leaf is applied to a surface which has been built up from layers of gesso, which is a white plaster-like substance, ochre and coloured burnish clay (red is a good choice), it can be rubbed with a burnishing stone to give it a high polish. This means that matt and burnished surfaces can be combined within one piece of work. In addition beautifully subtle effects can be achieved by 'distressing', ie rubbing back through the layers of leaf, clay and ochre.

Water gilding will not, however, withstand the elements and cannot be used for exterior work.

The process of water gilding is a fairly lengthy one and demands care and patience, but the results which can be achieved are well worth the time and perseverance spent mastering the techniques.

To experiment with water gilding buy some wooden moulding from a timber yard—inexpensive, door frame mould-ing was used to make the picture frame in the photographs.

The method described here is for water gilding wood. Tips for dealing with metal and glass are given at the end of the chapter.

Preparing the surface

New wood should be rubbed down with glasspaper or flour paper to give a smooth surface and then dusted off. No more preparation is needed.

Painted wood. All paint must be removed with paint stripper and wire wool, neutralized according to the instructions on the can, dried and then rubbed down with glasspaper or flour paper if necessary.

Gilded wood. If you wish to replace damaged gilding on a piece you must strip it back to the gesso. Use paint stripper for this, neutralize and dry. Apply more gesso if necessary. You can then apply ochre and burnish clay.

You will need:

Tools as for oil gilding (Gilding chapter 2, page 1648), plus burnishing stone.

No.8 or No.10 hog hair brushes.

Earox (ox-hair) or sable brushes.

Tins, small bowls, screw-top jars.

2 washing-up bowls.

Medium-sized strainer.

2 nylon tea strainers.

Metal bucket or large saucepan.

Flour paper or Lubersil paper (extra-fine abrasive papers) and glasspaper.

Rabbit skin size and gilder's whitening powder (both available from art shops and decorators' suppliers).

Ochre gouache (ochre golden, ground in water with 10% chrome yellow) is a good colour to use and can be bought in tubes and jars ready to use.

Burnish clay (bole) which can be bought in solid cones.

Precious leaf.

Methylated spirit.

Pumice powder (if you wish to distress the surface).

Rabbit skin size

Rabbit skin glue, made from animal cartilage and skin, is obtainable in granular form. It is mixed with water and used for priming and 'putty' and, in decreasing strengths, is used as the basis for mixing gesso, ochre, burnish clay and laying water (see chart, fig.1).

To make up full-strength size. In a metal container (large tin), soak 283 gm (10oz) granules of rabbit skin glue in 568ml (1 pint) cold water for about half an hour. Stir occasionally to allow size to absorb water.

Add boiling water to make up 3.12 litres (5½ pints). Place tin in a large saucepan or metal bucket containing water. Simmer on stove or gas ring for about an hour. Stir occasionally.

When cold the size will set to form a rubbery substance (as will gesso and other substances with which size is mixed). When needed, a piece of size is cut off and rendered down over heat in a tin placed in a pan of water.

Note: all the substances described here containing size are rendered down in this way (if they have set) or the size will burn.

Size kept in a cool place will last for up to four days. When it is 'off' it will smell and turn back into liquid. Do not use size in this condition.

Priming. Brush a coat of hot, full-strength size all over the work to prime it. If you add a tablespoonful of gilder's whitening to the size it will give just enough colour to ensure that you cover every part of the work. When this primer is dry, rub down the surface with flour paper.

'Putty'. If there are small faults in the surface, eg nail holes, these can be made good with gilder's putty. This is done by simply mixing a little gilder's whitening to make a putty-like paste with a few drops of hot, full-strength size. This is best used as soon as it is made.

When the putty is dry, rub down the surface with a medium-grade glass-paper. If you find you have rubbed off some of the primer, give the whole surface another coat.

Before applying gesso, dust off the surface to remove any grit or dust.

Gesso

Gesso is a white liquid made from gilder's whitening mixed with diluted size.

To make up gesso. In a washing-up bowl, mix two parts size with one part boiling water. Add gilder's whitening to the hot size mixture until gesso reaches the consistency of thin batter.

Note: keep some of this diluted size for thinning and 'topping up' gesso.

Pour gesso from one bowl to the other through a medium-sized strainer.

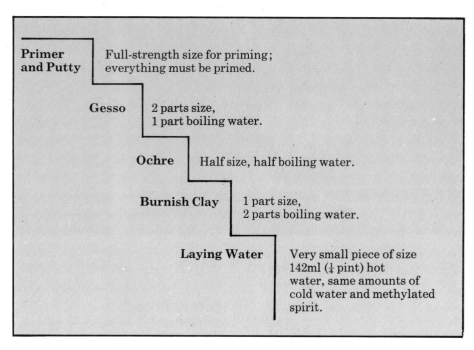

Primer and Putty	Full-strength size for priming; everything must be primed.
Gesso	2 parts size, 1 part boiling water.
Ochre	Half size, half boiling water.
Burnish Clay	1 part size, 2 parts boiling water.
Laying Water	Very small piece of size 142ml (¼ pint) hot water, same amounts of cold water and methylated spirit.

1. *Chart shows strength of size for the various processes.*

Repeat the process four or five times until gesso is really smooth.

Test the gesso on a piece of carving. If it is too thick it will clog the carving. Add some reserve size to correct it.

Applying gesso. Gesso is applied at blood heat, using a number 8 or 10 hog hair brush. Keep gesso warm by putting container into bucket of hot water occasionally.

Apply one coat of gesso, first brushed on and then stippled. Stippling the surface will ensure the high points on the carving take gesso easily and that gesso does not build up in the crevices. Allow surface to dry.

Apply a second coat, stippling on the gesso and then brushing lightly over the surface to smooth it. Leave to dry. Repeat first and second applications three or four times and then repeat

second application three or four times. As you work you may find that, due to evaporation, the gesso thickens. Thin it with the reserved size—it is most important that the strength of the gesso remains constant.

If, in between coats, you notice small defects rub them down with flour paper. When you are happy with your gessoed surface rub it over with flour paper. Then wash the surface with a mixture of equal parts of methylated spirit and cold water—use a stubby brush for the crevices.

Ochre

Preparing ochre. Mix one part size with one part boiling water. Pour a little into a mixing bowl. Then put about a tablespoonful of ochre gouache on the inside of the bowl, near the top. Next, with a clean hog hair brush, gradually mix the ochre gouache into the size. Try to dissolve the ochre

Simmer size as described. In the foreground are dry and soaked granules and cold, set size.

Pour gesso through strainer four or five times to ensure it is smooth and free of lumps.

Apply gesso, keeping it at blood heat by putting container into bucket of hot water occasionally.

Geoffrey Frosh

Gradually mix ochre gouache into hot size to form a thin paste. Then strain it through a fine strainer.

Paint a coat of hot ochre over whole surface. Allow to dry, rub lightly with flour paper and brush off dust.

gouache evenly into the size to form a thin paste.

With a hog hair brush paint a little colour on to a spare piece of wood. If the colour is too dense, add more size; if it is too insipid, add more ochre. When you have a satisfactory colour, strain the ochre mixture through a very fine strainer to remove any grit.

Note: make up enough ochre for your whole piece of work.

Applying ochre. Paint a coat of hot ochre over the whole surface of the work. Allow it to dry and then rub lightly with flour paper and brush off dust. Keep the ochre hot as shown in the photograph.

Burnish clay (bole)

This clay can be bought in small, solid 'cones'. Place cone in a cloth and then hammer to crush it. Put crushed clay in a screw-top jar, and just cover with water and replace lid. It will be ready for use in about 24 hours.

Preparing the clay. Mix one part size with two parts boiling water. Mix up clay from the jar with size in a similar way to that used for mixing up ochre. Use a stiff brush and mix enough clay into the size to give a consistency which will drip off the brush. If it is too thin it will run through the brush and if too stiff it will stay on the bristles.

When you are satisfied with the consistency, strain burnish clay through a fine strainer.

Applying burnish clay. Use a sable or Earox (ox-hair) brush to paint on a thin coat of clay. Allow to dry. Repeat. When the clay is dry, rub surface with flour paper, then remove 'dead' clay with a stiff, clean, bristle brush and rub with a piece of velvet to give a good lustre. Paint over surface lightly with methylated spirit, to remove any excess grease which could have occurred by handling, concentrating on the crevices.

Water gilding

Laying water is made by dissolving a thumb nail sized piece of solid, full-strength size in 142ml ($\frac{1}{4}$ pint) of hot water, mixing in the same amount of cold water and of methylated spirit.

If you intend to have large matt surfaces on your finished gilded surface, paint over these surfaces only with laying water and allow to dry.

Laying the leaf. Turn out loose leaf, flatten, cut and pick up as for oil gilding.

Then wet the surface where first piece of leaf is to be laid with laying water, using a sable or Earox brush.

Lay the piece of leaf flat on the wet area. Leave for half a minute, then dab with your mop.

Lay the next piece of gold slightly overlapping the first. Dab the first piece with cotton wool and dab the second one with the mop after it has been down for half a minute. Repeat over the whole surface. Work from left to right if you are right-handed. Reverse the process if you are left-handed.

When you have finished, leave the piece of work to dry for between one and three hours. Rub surface over with mop and cotton wool to remove loose particles of gold.

Faulting. If you find the gold has 'missed' on any part of the surface, wet exposed area and lay gold as before. Check for faulting before and after burnishing.

Burnishing. When the work is dry it can be burnished. Hold the burnishing stone in one hand and guide it over the surface with the other.

Distressing the surface

To slightly distress the surface, simply paint on laying water over the leaf. This will take away some of the brightness of the gold.

To distress, rub the surface down with pumice powder and cotton wool. This will bring the clay and ochre colours through. (You can even expose part of the white, gessoed surface if you wish.) Dust the surface over with a brush, re-burnish and then coat entire surface with laying water.

Metal and glass

Metal. Cylindrical metal surfaces, like the arms of a light bracket, are the most practical to water gild. Shellac the surface to be gilded and allow to dry. Then, dip fine string or bandage in hot, thin gesso and bind it round your surface. Allow it to dry, putty the surface, rub it smooth. Then apply gesso, ochre, burnish clay and leaf as usual.

Flat surfaces must be coated with shellac before a piece of linen soaked in thin hot gesso is pressed down on to the surface.

It is not practical to water gild an intricate relief surface as much detail would be obscured by the linen.

Glass. The gold leaf is applied from the back on to thoroughly cleaned glass.

If possible prop up the sheet of glass at an angle of about 45° and stand it on small blocks of wood. This ensures that the laying water runs freely down the glass and does not collect at the base, possibly damaging the leaf.

Lay gold as previously described, laying full leaves where possible and only overlapping slightly.

When gold is dry, bring a kettle of water to the boil, plug the spout with a piece of wood with a small hole through it and direct the thin jet of steam from this on to the gold. Start at the top and play the jet of steam across the glass from one side to the other. You will see the water that is still between the glass and gold 'liven up' and start to run down the glass. Follow water down with jet of steam until you reach the bottom of glass. This gives a mirror-like finish to the gold. Protect the back of the gold with clear varnish.

Mix up clay with stiff hog hair brush. In foreground are a cone of clay, a crushed cone and an ox-hair brush.

Paint on two thin coats of warm burnish clay, using a sable or ox-hair brush. Allow surface to dry between coats.

When clay is dry, rub surface with flour paper, then remove 'dead' clay with a stiff, clean, bristle brush.

Lay each piece of leaf flat on area wetted with laying water. Successive pieces of gold overlap slightly.

Burnish the work. Hold the burnishing stone in one hand and guide it over the surface with the other.

This antique carved bird is a particularly fine example of the technique of water gilding.

Dick Miller

Lost wax casting for jewelry

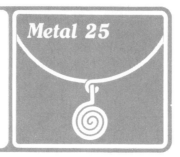
To illustrate the method of lost wax casting described in the previous metal chapter, the steam and vacuum systems of drawing the metal into the mould have been chosen. They are both simple versions and kits are readily available from craft suppliers.

The wax model

Two simple objects, a ring and a pendant, are used as the wax models. Equipment needed for all stages of casting is listed in box, opposite.

The ring. To cast a ring, a wax model or 'blank' is needed. This can be bought or made. To make one, mark a distance of 2.5cm (1″) from either end of a strip of aluminium or tin sheeting (fig.A). Fold these two marked off ends towards each other.

☐ Bend the sheet to form an arch shape so that the two folded end pieces overlap (as shown in fig.B opposite). Fasten the ends with masking tape. This forms the outer casing into which the wax for the model is poured. A hole in the centre for your finger is made by placing the mandril in the mould before pouring the wax (fig.C).

☐ Place the aluminium casing on a

Below: silver jewelry made using the lost wax method. The pendant piece is polished with a small, electric polisher. Designer: G. Leybourn-Needham.

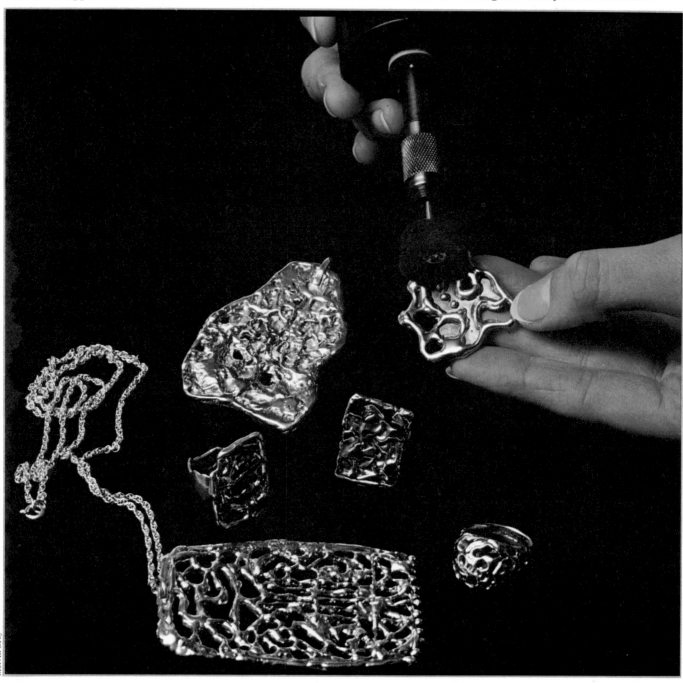

Melvin Grey

flat surface with plasticine around the base. This prevents the molten wax from leaking out of the casing. Stand the mandril upright in the centre of the casing and pour the molten wax (fig.C).

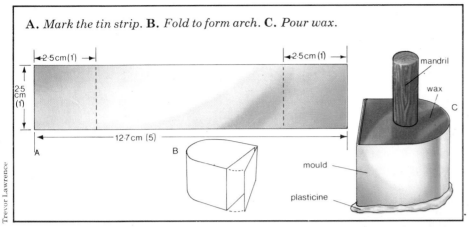

A. *Mark the tin strip.* B. *Fold to form arch.* C. *Pour wax.*

☐ To ensure that the wax does not stick to the mandril and flat surface, spray them first with the release agent.

☐ Remove the wax from the mould by dipping the mould into hot water. The wax should melt just enough to slide out of the mould. You are now left with a wax ring model, called a 'blank'. The ring blank can now be carved and decorated using the spatulas and sharp knife.

The pendant piece. First draw the required design on a piece of paper.

☐ Place a sheet of transparent wax over the design and, using a tjanting (or similar wax pen), build up the areas that you want to stand out from the background—the light area on the drawing (fig.1).

☐ Burn out the areas with a hot knife where you do not want any metal (dark areas in the picture). Cut out the whole design when the wax is dry and you are left with the wax model of the pendant you want to reproduce in metal.

1. *Place a sheet of wax over the pendant design and trace over with wax. Build up some areas with a wax pen.*

Tools and materials

Model making: an alcohol lamp, modelling spatulas and tools, pencil and paper, a sharp knife, old coarse files and medium grade glasspaper, ring mandrils or dowels, wax pen (batik tjanting) or welder, a strip of aluminium sheet or tin plate 25mm (1″) wide and 12.7cm (5″) long, silicone furniture polish or a commercial release agent and plasticine.

Sprueing: rubber or metal sprue bases, 50mm to 75mm (2″ to 3″) wide with metal flasks to fit. Gram balance. Wax or metal sprues, 2mm ($\frac{1}{16}$″) and 1mm ($\frac{1}{32}$″) thick.

Investing: rubber or plastic mixing bowl, wooden or plastic spatula, measuring jug.

Burn-out: a small, electric muffle kiln, kiln tongs, asbestos gloves, pieces of firebrick and metal tray.

Casting: casting device—either a vacuum kit or a steam pressure system—blowtorch, bronze or copper tweezers and a heat-proof mat.

Recovery: plastic bucket, tongs, stiff brush and a solution of dilute sulphuric acid for the cleaning pickle.

Finishing: piercing saw, jeweller's files, emery sticks, rouge and tripoli sticks and buffs, portable battery drill.

2. *Attach sprues to model and mount on sprue base. On the left is a wax model of a ring fastened on to a sprue base.*

Sprueing

This is the procedure for attaching sprues down which the metal is forced into the mould (fig.2, previous page). The wax or metal sprues are joined to the wax model. Joins on wax are made by warming both surfaces with a hot spatula and then bringing them quickly together. Sticky wax may be used for joining but use it sparingly as it is difficult to remove excess wax without damaging the model. A clean heating flame from an alcohol lamp is essential for this.

The size and type of the wax wire used for the sprueing is important and depends on whether the vacuum or steam method of casting is used. The sprue holes should be big enough for the metal to go down only when it is forced: it should not drip down the hole. The correct size sprue wire ensures that the capillary action will keep the metal in the crucible depression until the casting force is applied.

For the hand vacuum system used here the wax sprue wire should be 2mm ($\frac{1}{16}''$) in diameter. For the steam system a 1mm ($\frac{1}{32}''$) metal wire should be used between the reservoir and the model. The reservoir, situated at the point where the sprues from the object merge, consists of a small ball of wax. One sprue joins this to the sprue base. In all cases the sprue from the reservoir to the crucible depression should be a 2mm ($\frac{1}{16}''$) wax wire.

Keep in mind that all parts of the wax model should be higher than the reservoir, as it is difficult for the molten metal to reverse its direction of flow when it is being drawn through into the mould.

After the model has been sprued and before the sprue base is attached, the model (and attached sprues) must be carefully weighed so that the amount of metal needed for the object can be estimated. If you do not have a gram balance a pharmacist will probably be able to weigh the object for you. Make a note of the weight so that when you come to casting, the amount of metal needed can be calculated.

The sprued model is then attached to the sprue base with the appropriate wax or metal main sprue wire. The whole model is dipped several times into the soapy liquid to prevent bubbles forming and allowed to dry completely.

Investing

☐ Place the metal flask on the sprue base so that the model is enclosed, making sure that no part of the model is closer than 6mm ($\frac{1}{4}''$) to the sides and top of the flask. Seal the bottom of the flask with plasticine.

☐ Mix the investment according to the manufacturer's instructions. Avoid vigorous stirring as this creates

3. *If you have used a metal sprue wire to attach the model to the sprue base, remove it with a pair of pliers.*

bubbles in the investment and causes problems with the casting. The investment should begin to harden within eight minutes, so work quickly and carefully.

☐ When a smooth, creamy consistency has been reached pour the investment slowly down the side of the flask gradually filling it from the bottom upwards and displacing all trapped air. (Air bubbles caused during investing will form balls of metal on the casting.) The investment is levelled and left to dry before continuing.

Investment attracts moisture from the air so store in an air-tight container. Due to its short shelf life it is more practical for the amateur to buy it in small portions.

☐ Leave the flask and investment to dry for one hour. The sprue base can then be twisted or prised off and any excess investment cleared away from the edges of the flask.

The flask now has a depression in the investment where the sprue base was; this is the crucible depression in which the metal is melted.

☐ If a metal sprue has been used this is now carefully withdrawn (fig.3).

Lost wax casting now enters its final stages. The invested flask is ready for the burn-out—that is the removal of the wax from inside the investment. This is done by heating the mould in a kiln.

The burn-out

The burn-out process is always started with a cold kiln and a damp, invested flask.

The burn-out process achieves several things. It eliminates from the investment all traces of the wax model and

sprue system—the wax is 'lost' from the mould—and dries out the mould.

The process also serves to raise the temperature of the mould to the correct temperature of the metal to be cast. For this reason the burn-out and casting stages are inseparable.

If, by some chance, your invested flask has dried out you may be able to remedy the situation by leaving the flask in a bowl of water for an hour before the burn-out.

The burn-out process can be divided into two parts, namely, eliminating the wax and heating the mould to the temperature required for casting.

Eliminating the wax. Place the flask, sprue hole downwards, into a cold kiln. Rest the flask on two small pieces of firebrick. This allows the air to circulate under the flask and the wax to run out.

☐ To keep the floor of the kiln clean or to retain the wax for subsequent cleaning and re-use, place the pieces of firebrick on a metal tray.

☐ Switch on the kiln and heat to a low temperature—about 150°C (302°F)—and keep it there for an hour.

Heating the mould. Using the kiln tongs and asbestos gloves, remove the tray leaving the flask still standing on the firebricks.

☐ Over the next 1½ hours, bring the heat of the kiln up to maximum temperature.

If your kiln is fitted with input controllers or a full temperature control, divide the range into about four steps. Simple kilns without controls should be left to heat up with the door slightly open—about 25mm (1"). This prevents a too rapid temperature rise.

☐ Half way through this cycle, using tongs and asbestos gloves, turn the flask upright, ie sprue hole on top.

☐ The flask is ready for casting when the sprue hole is bright red and the surrounding investment is bone white.

Casting

The casting follows immediately after the invested flask has been taken from the kiln. If the flask cools excessively and needs to be reheated, cracks will occur in the investment. Therefore, have all the equipment at hand before the flask is withdrawn from the kiln. The amount of metal needed must be calculated before the flask is removed. This can be done, as follows, during the heating of the mould.

Weighing the metal. The metal weight is needed to determine how much must be melted for casting. To calculate this weight, the specific gravity (SG) of the metal and wax must be known.

The SG of most waxes used in this process is between 0.8 and 0.95. It is sufficient to say 1.0 for our calculations.

Melvin Grey

4. *The steam casting system. As soon as the metal is ready, the blowtorch is removed and the hand-held section of the caster placed firmly on top of the flask.*

5. *The vacuum casting system. By pulling out the handle, pressure is reduced below the mould; atmospheric pressure on top then forces the metal down into the mould.*

The SG of sterling silver is about 10.4 but take it as 11.0 for convenience. So, if you are casting with silver, multiply the weight of the wax model plus sprues (see previous metal chapter) by 11.0. Increase this weight by 15% to account for metal left in the crucible depression. This total is the amount of sterling silver you will need to melt in the crucible depression of the flask.

If you are using student's alloy, the SG of this is 8.69—take it as 9.0. Multiply this by the weight of the wax model and sprues, increase the figure by 15% and you have the weight of the metal necessary to fill the mould.

Steam casting. This is one method of forcing the metal into the mould. The caster consists of two sections; the base, on which the flask is placed during casting, and the handle which is pressed down on top of the flask. Soak the asbestos pad situated in the handle of the steam caster and leave to drain of excess water.

☐ Remove the heated flask from the kiln, remembering to use the asbestos gloves for protection. Place the hot flask on the dry asbestos pad in the base of the steam caster.

☐ Light the blowtorch and bring the flame to the depression.

☐ Place the correct weight of metal in the crucible depression, add a couple of pinches of powdered flux, and melt the metal.

☐ The metal is ready to be cast when it appears to spin round in the depression following the torch flame.

☐ Add another pinch of the flux to clear the metal surface.

☐ As soon as the metal starts spinning again, remove the blowtorch and quickly place the top of the steam

caster firmly and squarely over the flask (fig.4).

☐ Press down for one minute. This serves to force the metal down the sprue hole to take up the shape originally occupied by the wax model inside the investment.

Vacuum casting. This is an alternative method to steam casting. The basic procedure is as follows.

☐ Clamp the vacuum caster to the edge of a table. Test to see that it is clamped firmly by placing your thumb over the small hole in the top and pulling the handle. This will also give you some idea of the vacuum strength.

☐ Place the neoprene washer on the device so that it encircles the small hole. This washer, on which the flask stands, forms an air-tight seal between the flask and caster.

☐ Remove the hot flask and place it on the washer.

☐ With the blowtorch proceed to melt the metal as for the steam caster.

☐ When the metal is ready, pull the handle of the kit and hold it out for one minute. Keep the blowtorch on the metal button which should still be visible at this stage (fig.5).

☐ After one minute remove the flask from the caster and place it upright on a heatproof mat or surface for a further two minutes. This is to ensure that the metal has solidified.

If the crucible depression is clear of metal then the cast has been successful.

Recovery

At this stage the surrounding investment is cleaned from the casting. Using the tongs pick up the flask and gradually immerse it in a bucket of cold water. The investment will crack

and cause clouds of steam but leave the flask immersed.

After a few minutes the investment will disintegrate, leaving the casting free. Clean out the flask and clean the remaining investment off the casting with a stiff brush.

Pickling. This gives the casting a thorough cleaning, dissolving all the oxides and flux.

☐ Place the object in a pickle solution of dilute sulphuric acid—one part acid to ten parts water—which can be mixed by a pharmacist or bought from jewelry suppliers.

Note: this pickle solution is only used to clean sterling silver or student's alloy.

Finish

If sterling silver or student's alloy is used not much finishing is needed. One of the advantages of lost wax casting is that a very clean finish is achieved without having to laboriously polish the object.

Trimming. Remove the article from the pickle using a small pair of tongs.

☐ Wash it thoroughly in soapy water.

☐ Using a piercing saw cut off the sprues, reservoir and sprue button.

☐ With a succession of No.2 jeweller's files, emery sticks and hand buffs of tripoli and rouge, clean up and polish the casting. Tripoli and rouge are abrasive materials which are applied with a buff which is made from a strip of leather or felt attached to a handle. The job is simplified if you have a small, battery-powered drill with polishing attachments as the one shown on page 1838. These drills are available in kit form, complete with a wide range of fittings.

Dressing the table loom

The table loom and its very special vocabulary was introduced in Weaving chapter 22, page 1810. Threading up a table loom may look an imposing task to the beginner but, in fact, if you have followed the instructions on making a warp and threading up the roller loom in Weaving chapter 21, page 1784, you are well on your way to designing your own exclusive fabrics.

The poncho

This is an excellent first project to make on a table loom as it is simply made up from two perfectly straight pieces of weaving (fig.1). The design, shown in the photograph, is in plain weave and made up from botany wool for warmth and extra softness. As you get more proficient and confident about weaving on a table loom, you will be able to create garments in more complex weaves and patterns.

You will need:
50gm (2oz) pale blue 3-ply wool.
250gm (9oz) navy blue 3-ply wool.
75gm (3oz) green 3-ply wool.
Four-shaft table loom with a 12 dent reed and a weaving width of at least 45cm (18″).
Stick or boat shuttle.
Warping pegs and G-clamps or warping board.
Threading hook and reed hook.
At least 12 warp sticks 15mm x 6mm (⅝″x ¼″) by the width of the warp beam on the inside of the frame.
Raddle.
Cotton twine or strong string and scissors.
Stiff brown paper.
Tape measure.

The loom. With many of the later weaving chapters, the basic four-shaft 60cm (24″) width loom is used as a model. If you have a loom that is wider or with more shafts you obviously have no problems and instructions are given throughout this chapter to guide you on your way. However, if you have a loom which is narrower than the weaving width of an article—45cm (18″) for the poncho—you will have to weave in strips and sew them together to make the pattern pieces. This will obviously be less successful. If you have a two shed roller loom as shown in Weaving chapter 21, page 1784, you can still make up the poncho as plain weave only needs the two sheds. Follow the instructions on threading the roller loom that are given in Weaving chapter 21 and ignore those that appear in this chapter which directly relate to the four-shaft loom. Remember that the rigid heddle has 13 not 12 dents per 2.5cm (1″) and extra threads will have to be warped to make up the total number of threads for the required width.

The pattern. To make the poncho you will need to weave two wool pieces of identical size. For an adult this would be two pieces 45cm x 82cm (18″x 32½″) when taken off the loom.
If you wish to alter the size, be very careful to alter all the instructions relating to numbers of threads and heddles on each shaft.
As the pattern for the warp threads is completely plain and exactly the same in both pieces, only one warp needs to be put on the loom and the two pieces woven in succession with a 25cm (10″) gap between them.

The warp

The final length of each piece of weaving is 82cm (32½″). To compensate for take up on the loom and shrinkage with washing, the 'weaver's yard' must actually be woven. This means that for each 91cm (36″) of weaving, 10cm (4″) extra must be woven to allow for this shrinkage. Therefore, each pattern piece of the poncho needs an extra 9cm (3½″) of weaving and each pattern piece will actually be woven 91cm (36″) long.
In addition, 45cm (18″) must be added to the warp for tying up and for the area which cannot be woven beyond the reed. The poncho also needs some warp for fringing at one end of each piece of weaving. Add on another 25cm (10″) fringing before the first piece of weaving. The fringe at the end of the second piece can be made out of warp waste beyond the reed.
Finally, a gap of about 25cm (10″) must be left between the two pieces of weaving.
Therefore, for the poncho you will need a warp of 82cm (32½″) plus 82cm (32½″) plus 18cm (7″) for actual weaving, plus 45cm (18″) for tying up and the warp that cannot be woven beyond the reed, 25cm (10″) for fringing and 25cm (10″) for the gap between the two pieces of weaving. This gives a total of 277cm (110″).

Width of warp. The weaving pieces are 45cm (18″) wide and the reed is 12 ends per 2.5cm (1″). The number of threads will be 12 multiplied by 18 which is 216. In addition, this particular design has a firm selvedge. To achieve this you will need not one but three extra threads on each side. Therefore, the total number of warp threads is 216 plus 6 making 222.

Making the warp. Make a warp of 222 threads each 277cm (110″) long. (See Weaving chapter 21, for full instructions of making a warp using warping pegs.)
Although it is perfectly feasible to make a warp of this length using warping pegs and a table, you may prefer to invest in a proper warping board that can either be kept flat or hung on a wall (fig.2). This piece of equipment makes it possible to make

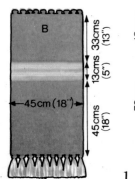

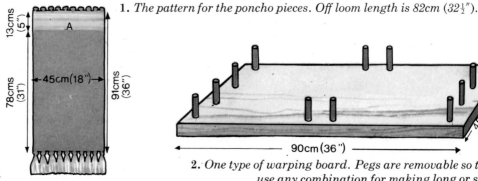

1. *The pattern for the poncho pieces. Off loom length is 82cm (32½″).*

2. *One type of warping board. Pegs are removable so that you can use any combination for making long or short warps.*

Coral Mula

This soft wool poncho is made up from two straight pieces of weaving. Designed by Melanie McKennell.

1843

very long warps as well as short ones without monopolizing vast areas of the kitchen table. The dowel pegs in the board are removable and the journey of the warp can be extended by winding it around extra pegs.

Raddle cross. As well as making the all-important cross in the warp that gives you the under/over sequence when threading, you may also find it helpful to make another cross at the opposite end of the warp. Make the cross in batches of six threads (fig.3), and your raddle threading will be a lot easier. If you do make the raddle or batch

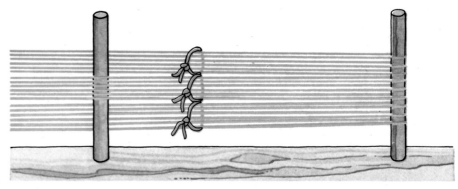

3. *By making a raddle cross it is easier to thread the raddle.*

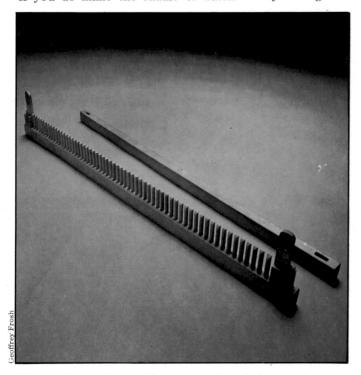

Geoffrey Frosh

The top of a wooden raddle prevents threads from escaping.

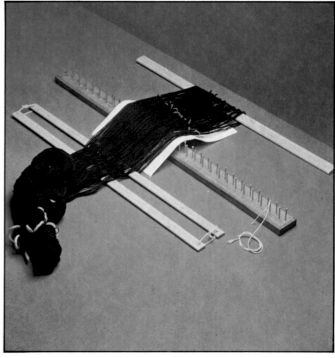

Putting the batches of threads in the raddle spaces.

cross, remember that the first and last groups of threads must contain the extra threads of the selvedge. Tie around each batch with cotton thread.

Putting on the warp. On a table loom with shafts it is advisable to use a proper wooden raddle. Ascertain the centre dent and count out to the dents 23cm (9″) each side of the centre. Mark these two dents with a piece of yarn. After inserting the warp stick and cross sticks, slide the cross sticks down the chained up warp and spread the intervening warp over the raddle protected by a piece of paper.

Thread the raddle from one of the dents you have marked, 23cm (9″) from the centre. This will ensure that the warp, and therefore the weaving, is centred so that the loom is kept balanced.

If you have made the raddle cross, you will find that each tied batch will slot into a dent which makes the process considerably quicker. Do not forget that the dent at each end must contain the three extra threads for the selvedge

so each end dent will have nine threads. Place the wooden top back in place on the raddle and tie around the raddle so that the top cannot slip off allowing the threads to become misplaced.

Move the warp to the loom with the warp stick at the warp beam end and the cross sticks on the warp beam side of the shafts. Tie the warp stick to the warp beam. Tie the raddle to the back frame of the loom so that the threads are brought from the beam over the frame, through the raddle and into the space between the shafts and the back frame.

Wind the warp little by little on to the warp beam and preferably with the help of a friend. One person should wind the beam while the other faces the loom and holds the threads in tension. The first section of warp must have warp sticks inserted to keep the warp evenly in tension. Always make sure that the sticks are directly on top of each other (fig.4). When you have used up all the sticks you can use

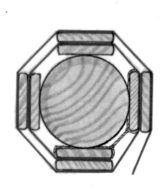

4. *Cross-section of the warp beam with the warp threads being wound on. Warp sticks should be inserted between the roller and the threads to keep the layers of threads separate and to prevent the unwoven warp from being distorted by the roller.*

of your four shafts. This will give you a total of 216 heddles, ie the correct number for your threads as the three selvedge threads merely double up.

Plain weave

Plain weave is simply over one/under one and therefore you need to thread up your loom so that you can alternately lift the odd and then the even threads.

To achieve plain weave on a four-shaft loom, the warp ends are threaded on to the shafts in the order 1, 2, 3, 4 and the shafts are then lifted in pairs. Shafts are numbered 1 to 4 from the front to the back of the loom. Shafts 1 and 3 lift all the odd threads and shafts 2 and 4 lift the even threads. Obviously, it is possible to produce other types of weave but these would require either a different lifting combination or a different threading.

The simplest method is to have all the odd numbered threads on the odd numbered shafts and the even threads on the even shafts.

Entering. To thread the heddles, face the loom and take the first two threads on the outside of the right-hand bunch off the cross sticks and thread them through the eye of the first heddle on shaft 1. The two threads form part of the selvedge.

Thread the next two threads through the first heddle on shaft 2 and the next two threads through the first heddle on shaft 3. These three sets of double threads form the selvedge.

Take the next thread off the cross sticks and thread through the first heddle on shaft 4. The next thread from the cross sticks should now go through the second heddle on shaft 1 and so on. Repeat across the warp, taking the threads in the correct order and threading them on to the shafts in a 1, 2, 3, 4 order (fig.5). Make sure that the threads come off the cross sticks in the correct order and that all the over threads go on to one pair of shafts while all the under threads go on to the other pair of shafts.

Threading hook. If you have difficulty

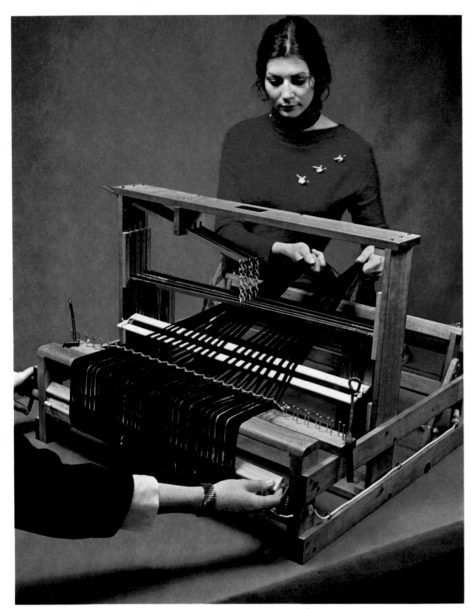

Rolling the warp on to the loom. One person should wind the warp while the other holds the warp in tension and clears any tangles that appear.

brown paper between the layers of threads as the warp is being wound on. If you have a large number of warp sticks do not use paper but put in further circuits of sticks after each two complete turns of the warp beam. Whether you use sticks or paper the idea is to keep the threads separate.

Stop winding the warp when it has completely unchained and you have only enough thread in front to go through the heddles and reed and to tie to the cloth beam. At this stage the cross sticks should be eased back through the warp until they are only about 5cm (2″) away from the back of the frame. Make sure that they remain in this position.

Divide the warp into two equal sections. Tie each half in an overhand knot and cut all the loops. As the

warping pegs bend inwards slightly as the warp is made, you will find that the last threads warped will be slightly shorter than the first. This means that you may find the warp is uneven. Trim down and even the warp, cutting off any knots that you may have tied. Before threading the heddles, make sure that you have 54 heddles on each

5. *Threads should be threaded on to the four shafts in turn.*

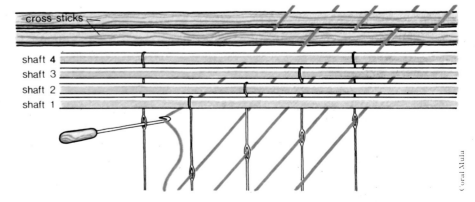

Using a hook to thread a heddle.

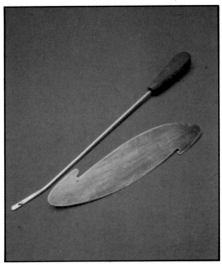

Threading hook and reed hook.

Geoffrey Frosh

A reed hook is used to sley the reed.

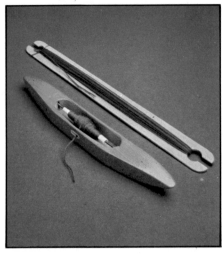

A boat shuttle with a stick shuttle.

threading the heddles with your fingers, a threading hook should be used instead. Push the hook through the eye of the heddle, catch your thread and pull it through.

When you have finished threading the right-hand bunch of threads start threading the left-hand bunch remembering to continue with the 1, 2, 3, 4 sequence. When you have only the last six outside threads left, thread them in pairs on to the last heddle on shafts 2, 3 and 4.

If you think that you have made a mistake in the threading up, check that you have not missed out either a thread or a shaft in the threading process.

The reed

The reed controls the sett or spacing of the threads just as the nails did on the tapestry frame. Because different setts are needed for different fabrics, reeds are available in different sizes. For the poncho a 12-dent reed is recommended. However, if you have a roller loom with a rigid heddle then the 13 dents per 2.5cm (1") of the heddle

will produce a slightly firmer fabric as there are more threads to each 2.5cm (1") square.

Reeds can be used for more than one spacing as threads can be doubled up or dents can even be missed out.

For instance, the 12-dent reed can be used for: 6 ends per 2.5cm (1") by threading every other dent; 12 ends—every dent; 18 ends—one thread and two threads alternately; 24 ends—two threads. If it can be avoided, try not to leave empty dents and it is strongly advised that you gradually build up a collection of reeds for different density fabrics.

Threading the reed. When all the heddles have been threaded, the warp has to be entered through the reed. This process is known as sleying and a special reed hook makes it easy.

Mark the centre of your reed and face the loom. Push the reed hook through the centre dent and pick up the centre thread on shaft 1.

Working in either direction, enter all the threads in the correct order of the shafts. Remember to follow the order

4, 3, 2, 1 from right to left and 1, 2, 3, 4 from left to right.

When you come to the last threads which have been threaded double through the heddles, treat them as one thread and place the doubled threads through one dent of the reed.

Tying on. When all the threads have been entered through the reed, tie the warp threads into groups of about twenty. Remove the raddle and tie the warp on to the front beam with the apron stick. It is very important to make sure that the warp is evenly tensioned across the full width.

Roll the cloth beam forward a little to even up the tension of the warp. Do not remove the cross sticks. Before you begin to weave, you should always check to see that you have threaded up correctly by lifting each pair of shafts in turn. Any thread that remains static has obviously not been threaded through a heddle. A tangle between the reed and heddle will result in the crossed threads remaining stationary and any mistakes in sleying the reed will be shown in unusually thick or thin areas of threads.

Check carefully for mistakes and make sure that they are corrected before weaving starts or you will have bad flaws in your fabric.

Weaving the poncho

As the poncho has a 25cm (10") fringe at the beginning, roll 30cm (12") of warp on to the cloth beam before starting to weave.

Shuttle. When working on a wider warp it is much quicker to weave with a proper boat shuttle, although a stick shuttle is perfectly sufficient.

The boat shuttle is shaped so that it can slide quickly through the shed when propelled by a push from one hand and caught by the other hand—hence the term 'throwing' the shuttle. Bobbins are contained within the boat shape and rotate as they play out the weft thread. These can be wound either by hand or with a proper bobbin winder but make sure that you do not overwind the bobbin.

☐ Wind up your shuttle or bobbin with the navy blue yarn.

☐ Pull the batten forward to clear the shed and return it.

☐ Raise shafts 1 and 3 and weave one pick.

☐ Raise shafts 2 and 4 and clear the shed with the batten once more.

☐ Weave one pick and beat down gently with the batten. Leave the loop as mentioned in Weaving chapter 21, page 1784 so that the weft yarn is not too tight.

☐ Change shed and clear with the batten before weaving the next pick.

☐ You will soon get into a rhythm of throwing the shuttle, beating down,

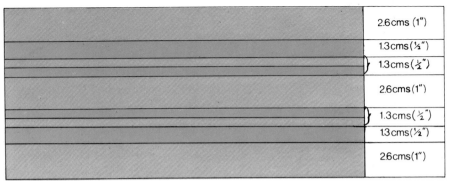

	2.6 cms (1")
	1.3 cms (½")
	1.3 cms (½")
	2.6 cms (1")
	1.3 cms (½")
	1.3 cms (½")
	2.6 cms (1")

6. *Detail of the striped area included in both pieces of the poncho.*

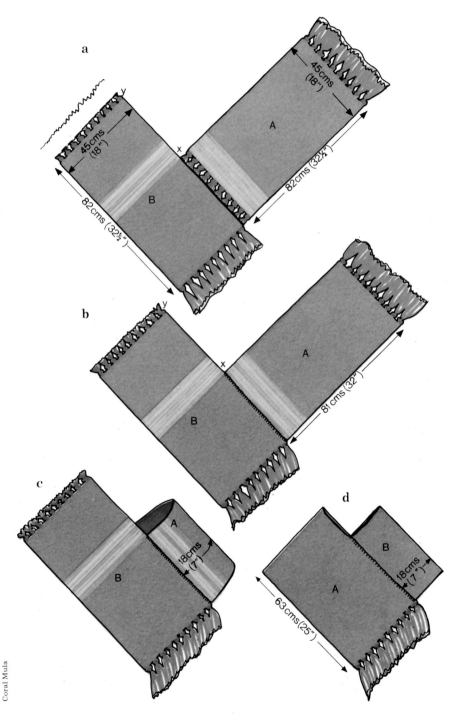

Coral Mula

7a-d. *The four stages in making up the poncho. Striped areas are on the front.*

changing shed, beating and throwing the shuttle again.

Try to keep the weave as balanced as possible by weaving roughly 11 picks per 2.5cm (1"). When the cloth is taken off the loom it should spring back to give you a perfectly balanced sett.

Weaving the pattern. The two pattern pieces have large areas of navy blue with a small 13cm (5") band of smaller blue and green stripes (see fig.1 and fig.6).

☐ For piece A (see fig.1) weave 78cm (31") in navy blue yarn. As you get close to the heddles, wind the woven cloth on to the cloth beam placing sticks in with the fabric to keep it smooth. When you run out of sticks use brown paper. Also remember to move the cross sticks backwards when winding on, to ensure that they do not crash into the shafts.

☐ Weave the last 13cm (5") in the striped pattern, the details of which is shown in fig.6.

☐ When you have woven this pattern area you have completed the 91cm (36") of the first pattern piece. Leave a gap of 25cm (10") and insert a stick into the shed created by any one shaft. This will secure the stick and you will have something to beat against.

☐ Start weaving again just above the stick and follow the pattern for piece B (see fig.1).

☐ Weave 45cm (18") in the navy blue yarn.

☐ Weave the 13cm (5") of the striped pattern.

☐ Finish piece B by weaving 33cm (13") in navy blue.

☐ When you have finished the second piece of weaving, unroll the cloth beam and untie the warp from the cloth stick.

☐ Remove remaining warp from the warp stick, cut the loops and slide the warp out of the heddles and reed.

☐ Cut the warp area exactly in the middle of the gap so that the same amount of fringe is left on each piece. Trim the warp at the other ends of the pieces to leave 15cm (10") lengths.

☐ Make overhand knots at each end of the poncho pieces.

Making up the poncho. The two pattern pieces are joined together so that only one set of fringes from each piece will show.

☐ Place the two pieces on a flat surface in the positions shown in fig.7a. Cut short the fringes at ends X and Y as these will not show.

☐ Blanket stitch the two pieces together at X as shown in fig.7b, overlapping piece A 1cm (½").

☐ Fold piece A back 18cm (7") from this seam (fig.7c).

☐ Turn the poncho wrong side up. Fold forward 19cm (7½") of piece B (fig.7d) and join B to A with blanket stitch again allowing a seam of 1cm (½"). Press gently before wearing.

Perspective— colour, detail light and shade

So far in the Design know-how chapters on perspective, only the shape and size of objects drawn in perspective have been considered. There are other aspects of drawing which can also be used to convey the impression of space and distance in a painting or drawing. Colour, detail and light, if used in the correct way, can enhance the perspective in a painting and make it look more convincing.

Colours are never as clear or bright in the distance as they are when seen close up. Even the brightest red will look paler and dustier if seen from a distance (fig.1). The colours in a painting must fit in with the perspective—if an object in the distance is painted a very bright colour, it will appear to be closer than it really is, and the perspective will be destroyed.

Look at a landscape painting, and you will see that hills in the distance are never as bright a green as the foreground, although they may actually be the same colour when viewed from the same distance. Similarly, the view from a tall building fades into grey in the far distance, even though there may be brightly coloured objects in the distance.

Light and shade can also be used to help the perspective in a drawing. The contrast between light and shade seems less clear in the distance than in the foreground and, similarly, objects in bright sunlight always appear brighter when close up than when far away. If your drawing has a lot of light and shade in it, make the shadows in the distance less contrasting than those in the foreground and this will help the perspective (fig.2).

Detail is the third aspect of drawing which, if used correctly, will help convey the impression of depth and distance. Objects in the foreground of a picture will obviously be seen more clearly, and therefore in greater detail. Thus, when drawing a row of houses, for example, the bricks will be clearly seen on the first few houses but, as they get further away, the houses will appear an overall brick colour and the individual bricks will not be seen.

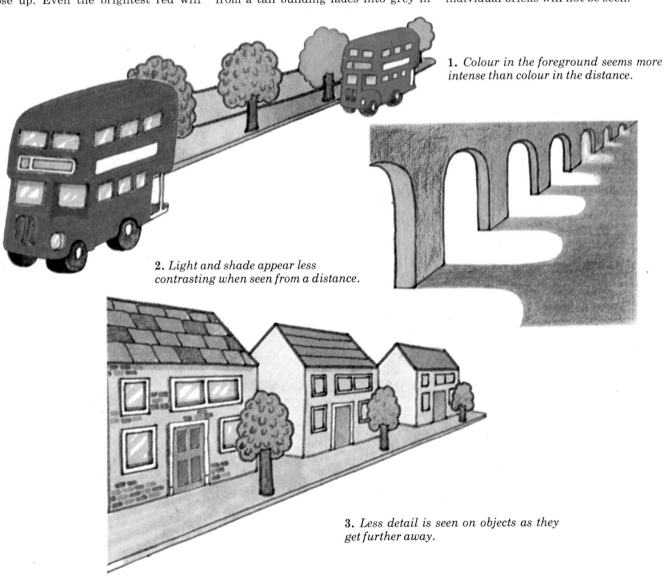

1. *Colour in the foreground seems more intense than colour in the distance.*

2. *Light and shade appear less contrasting when seen from a distance.*

3. *Less detail is seen on objects as they get further away.*

Creative ideas 66

Painted coat-hooks

Most homes have a shortage of coat-hooks—especially when they're also used for shoebags in the school holidays. Here is a way to solve the problem.

You will need:
Two pieces 13mm ($\frac{1}{2}''$) plywood, one 30cm (12") sq and one 35cm x 25cm (14"x 10").
Coping saw, drill with 6mm ($\frac{1}{4}''$) and 1.5mm ($\frac{1}{10}''$) drill bits and woodworking adhesive.
2 No.6 screws 3cm ($1\frac{1}{4}''$) long and 2 corresponding Rawlplugs.
Undercoat or wood primer.
Gloss paint.
2 pieces 6mm ($\frac{1}{4}''$) dowel, each 4cm ($1\frac{1}{2}''$) long.
Fine grade glasspaper or similar sandpaper.

Once you have decided which coat-hook you would like to make, draw your pattern from the graph, see fig.1.
Transfer to piece of 30cm (12") square plywood and cut out shape with coping saw. (For instructions on using a coping saw see Carpentry chapter 8, page 548.)
Smooth edges with glasspaper or sandpaper.
Prepare your shape with either undercoat or primer and then apply gloss paint. Decorate with either elephant features or football design, as shown.
To make back board. Taking your second piece of plywood, draw and trans-fer oval from graph, see fig.1.
Cut out with coping saw. Sand edges smooth.
Prime and paint.
Attaching coat-hook to back board. With 6mm ($\frac{1}{4}''$) drill bit drill two holes through back board, positioned as in fig.1. Holding coat-hook firmly in place against back board, mark positions for corresponding

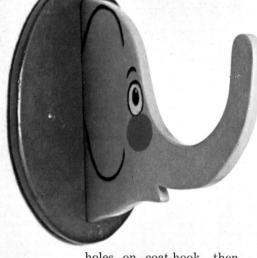

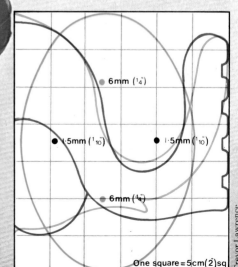

holes on coat-hook, then drill so that the total depth is about 4cm ($1\frac{1}{2}''$).
Apply glue to each piece of dowel and insert into the two holes to secure coat-hook to back board.
To attach back board to wall carefully drill two more holes through back board using 1.5mm ($\frac{1}{10}''$) drill bit and corresponding holes in the wall. Insert Rawlplugs into wall and firmly screw on finished coat-hook.

Eye-catching coat-hooks.

1. *Enlarge whichever shape is required from this graph pattern.*

6mm ($\frac{1}{4}''$)

1·5mm ($\frac{1}{10}''$)   1·5mm ($\frac{1}{10}''$)

6mm ($\frac{1}{4}''$)

One square = 5cm (2")sq

Trevor Lawrence

Teapot with clay or cane handle

One of the greatest potting challenges is to make a perfect teapot—an object which has both ritualistic and practical associations. We may no longer, in the West, regard tea as the precious gift of the gods, but the teapot is still an important part of the lives of many people.

This chapter explains how to make a basic teapot which can then be adapted into two distinct types, simply by the

Conventional side-handled and elegant cane-handled teapot, both designed by Emmanuel Cooper.

Paul Kemp

choice of handle. A side handle gives the pot a cosy, traditional look, while the top cane handle transforms it into an altogether more sophisticated affair. The design described here is wide-based, for stability, and holds about 1 litre (1½ pints). The lid is held in place by a flange which removes the necessity for making a galley seating on the body of the teapot and, therefore, helps to speed up production.

You will need:
A wheel.
A batt.
Bowl of water.
About 2kg (4lb) medium-soft prepared throwing clay.
Board.
Sponge on the end of a stick.
Turning tools.
Pointed wooden tool.
Sharp, thin-bladed knife.

Callipers.
Piercing tool (or old-fashioned pen knib in holder).
Two clean tiles (optional).

☐ Weigh the clay into the following approximate quantities: 1.25kg (2½lb) for the body; 250gm (½lb) for the lid; 142gm (5oz) for the spout; 28gm (1oz) for the knob; 250gm (½lb) for the handle or for the lugs for the cane handle.

The body

☐ Fix the batt on to the wheelhead (see Clay chapter 35, page 1542).
☐ Centre 1.25kg (2½lb) clay on the batt.
☐ Leave the centred clay with a wide base—about 15cm (6″) across.
☐ Open out the clay by the usual method, leaving a thickish base of about 2cm (¾″), and force the clay upwards to form walls (fig.1). Leave a good, thick roll at the top, pointing slightly inwards.

☐ Before pulling up the walls further, compress the clay of the base as described in Clay chapter 37, page 1658, using the flat part of the finger-tips.

☐ Bring up the walls of the pot with the fingers of the left hand inside and the fingers of the right hand outside. Aim to form a narrow-necked cone with a collared effect (fig.2).

☐ Use the finger-tips of the right hand to curve the top of the walls inwards over the left hand. Leave a roll of clay at the neck to give definition of shape as well as physical strength (fig.3).

Try to throw the walls in about four pulls because this will help to keep the clay fairly stiff and crisp. At this stage the neck should have a diameter of about 10cm (4″). If it spreads too wide, speed up the wheel and collar it in. Working with the recommended quan-

tity of clay, the thrown pot should be about 13cm (5″) tall and have a neck width of 8cm (3″). If it is smaller than this it means you have made a heavy pot in proportion of size to weight. You may be able to pull up the walls further but at this stage it is difficult and if the pot is too small and heavy it may be better to abandon it and start again. If, on the other hand, the pot is much larger than the suggested size, the walls or base are almost certainly too thin and, again, there is little you can do except set the clay aside for re-wedging and begin again.

☐ If the proportions are acceptable, mop out the inside of the pot, using a small soft sponge—attached to the end of a stick if necessary (fig.4).
☐ If you can get your fingers inside the pot without damaging the neck, smooth over the base after sponging.
☐ Use a wooden tool to trim any surplus clay from the base of the pot.
☐ Carefully measure the diameter of the opening for the lid and, finally, pass a cutting wire under the pot before removing the batt from the wheel.

The lid

This is thrown upside down, directly on to the wheelhead.
☐ Centre 250gm (½lb) of the clay and leave it in a rough mushroom shape, slightly narrower at the base (fig.5).
☐ Open out the middle.

Nelson Hargreaves

□ Support the edge underneath with the right hand and press downwards on the top edge with the left hand to form the outside lid edge (fig.6).

By now, the shape is almost formed.

□ Pull up the walls to form the flange, which should be about 12mm ($\frac{1}{2}$") high to fit snugly in the pot (fig.7).

□ Finish off the edge of the lid with the pointed wooden tool.

□ Use the callipers to check that the width of the flange will fit snugly into the neck of the pot.

□ Bring the edge of the lip upwards so that it will lie securely on the body of the teapot (fig.8).

□ Use the wooden tool to trim away surplus clay.

□ Pass the cutting wire between the lid and the wheelhead and place the lid on the board to dry out.

The spout

Successful spout making is a question of practice, but there are three points to bear in mind. First, use well-wedged clay, much softer than usual. Secondly, throw with a faster wheelhead speed than usual, because you are working in the very centre of the wheel. Thirdly, remember that unsightly throwing rings will be produced if you pull up too quickly.

□ Centre the 142gm (5oz) of clay in the usual way, and open it up right down to the wheelhead, because no base is necessary.

Do not allow the clay to spread out at the top—keep it tapering in as much as possible.

□ Bring up the walls, using the index finger of the left hand as an inside support (fig.9).

□ Collar in the spout, using plenty of water and keeping the index finger of the left hand inside as a support.

□ The walls can be brought up further when the top is narrow by inserting a thin wooden tool down the spout and throwing over this with the fingers of the right hand (fig.10).

Only with experience will you successfully judge the shape of the spout to suit your teapot. For this particular design, it should be about 5cm (2") wide at the base and about 8cm (3") long. Bear in mind that it should not be too open at the top or the tea will cool quickly.

□ Smooth outside with wooden tool before removing spout from the wheel.

Assembling the teapot

When the pieces are leather hard, they can be assembled. The less handling involved in this operation, the greater the chance of keeping the finished piece crisp and clean.

□ Turn the body as usual, supporting it on a chuck (see Clay chapter 36, page 1570). Leave a foot ring so that the base can be glazed and thereby strengthened.

□ Turn the lid.

□ Throw a knob on to the lid using no more than 28gm (1oz) of soft clay (see Clay chapter 37, page 1658).

□ Pierce a hole in the lid so that air can get into the pot as the tea is poured out.

□ Pierce a hole up from the inside of the lid, into the knob, so that any trapped air will be released.

When considering the best position for the spout it is helpful to regard it as an extension of the body and to place it accordingly. Style and individual preference will affect this decision, but, traditionally, the spout is placed low on the pot so that the water passes through the tea leaves as it is poured. Remember that the end of the spout should be higher than the maximum level of the teapot.

☐ Once the position has been decided, cut the spout at an angle of about 45° with a sharp, thin-bladed knife (fig.11).

☐ Place the spout in position and, with clean cuts, trim the join until the spout lies flush on the body.

☐ Dip the bottom of the spout in water and hold it against the body to leave a damp registration mark.

☐ Scratch the two surfaces to be joined.

☐ Pierce as many straining holes as possible (fig.12). Many holes ensure a good force of liquid in the spout which will improve flow and reduce drips.

☐ Paint the two surfaces to be joined with slip and press them firmly together.

☐ Smooth over the outside join.

☐ Trim the end of the spout as shown (fig.13). This allows for it to twist slightly in the firing.

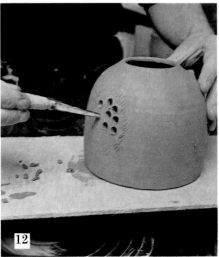

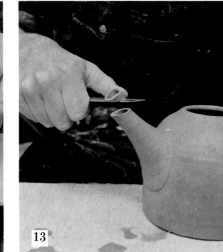

Handles

At this stage you must decide which teapot you intend to make.

Side handle. For a side-handled teapot, use the remaining 250gm (½lb) of clay to pull and attach a handle as described in Clay chapter 31, page 1346. Make sure that you place the handle directly opposite the spout and that the curve is wide enough to admit the fingers of one hand so that the pot is comfortable to hold when pouring.

Cane handle. Use the 250gm (½lb) of clay to make the lugs to hold the cane handle.

☐ Roll out two lengths of clay, each about 8cm (3″) long and 6mm (¼″) in diameter. You may find that the easiest way to do this is to roll the clay between two clean, damp tiles.

☐ When the length and diameter are right, press gently downwards with the top tile to flatten the lugs slightly.

☐ Scratch two join marks on the pot for each lug, about 4.5cm (1¾″) apart, setting one above the spout and the other directly opposite.

Be sure to set them sufficiently far away from the lid so that they do not impede its removal.

☐ Use slip to paint the areas to be joined.

☐ Press the lugs firmly into place.

☐ Use finger-tips to blend in the join.

Fettling

Whichever pot you have made, it must now be fettled inside and out, which means that any surplus pieces of clay must be scraped away with a turning tool and the pouring holes cleaned out with the pointed tool.

Glazing

When glazing any article of domestic ware, always bear in mind the safety precautions set out in Clay chapter 38, page 1745.

Both the pots illustrated were dipped completely, upright, in a white matt dolomite glaze, composed of felspar, dolomite and clay. They were then turned upside down and shaken thoroughly so that the surplus poured down the spout and cleared the pouring holes.

Attaching cane handle

The cane handle, which can be bought from any pottery supplier, cannot be attached until the pot has been fired. The handle is designed in such a way that it is very easy to attach. Be sure to soak it in water for a few minutes first, to make it pliable (fig.14).

Nelson Hargreaves

Hand-coloured photographs

Hand-coloured photographs are often thought to be old fashioned because before colour processes were developed, this was the only way of adding colour to a photograph.

Most people will have seen the early, tinted photographs on First World War postcards of famous actresses and sentimental scenes. Ordinary view postcards, too, were hand coloured until quite recently.

Today hand colouring is not just used as a substitute for colour photography but is an art in its own right. It is not necessary to colour an old picture; it can be interesting to work on any recent picture and enliven it with colour. The great advantage of hand colouring is that it need bear little resemblance to reality—a dismal day can become a sunset scene.

The picture that you colour is a matter of personal choice, there is really no limit to the subject: people, landscapes, buildings are all suitable. It is, however, usually preferable if the composition of the picture is fairly simple—for example, one person instead of a crowd.

There are different styles of colouring just as there are different styles of painting. You may want a bright, kitsch, postcard effect, or perhaps you prefer something more subtle and complementary to the subject to convey naturalism. You may want to emphasize small areas of a photograph with colour, or wash it over the whole picture. It is up to you.

The paper surface

It is possible to work on a photograph which has almost any finish. If you print the photograph yourself, however, you will be able to choose the paper with the best surface for hand colouring or, you may be able to arrange to have your pictures printed on a paper of your choice.

In general the more matt or textured the surface the better—Semi-matt, Kentmere, Kodalith, or a lustre finish paper, are suitable. If you are doing your own printing, print on a double-weight paper to avoid kinking when colour is applied.

Sepia toning (dyeing the photographic image brown) will give colours which are put on top a warmer look than when colouring a black and white print.

☐ Mix up a solution of 50gm (1½oz) potassium ferricyanide, 50gm (1½oz) potassium bromide and enough cold water to make up 1 litre (1¾ pints).

Photograph taken by Susan Wilks and hand coloured by her. The picture was sepia-toned first and then parts of it were coloured using the water-based method described here.

Susan Wilks

Pour this solution into a photographic developing tray and bleach your black and white print in it for five minutes.

☐ Leave print in tray and wash under cold running water for five to ten minutes, until all yellow has gone.

☐ Mix up a solution of 10gm ($\frac{1}{3}$oz) sodium sulphide (crystal or flake) and enough cold water to make 1 litre ($1\frac{3}{4}$ pints). Pour solution into developing tray. Place print in this toning bath and leave for two or three minutes. Wash print as before, blot between newspapers and leave to dry face-up on more newspaper. The print may curl but can be flattened when dry.

☐ All utensils (which should be kept for photographic use) and hands must be washed after using this process.

Water-based method

Water-based, soluble inks, such as Dr. Martins, Johnsons, Luma or Pelikan, obtainable from art shops, can be used. If there are to be large flat areas of colour, it is advisable to soak the print in cold water for about ten minutes, then dry off excess moisture with blotting paper. The print is now ready to work on. It is much easier to work on large areas in this way as the ink will spread on the damp surface leaving soft muted edges.

You must, however, be very careful to paint with the ink sufficiently diluted, as the colour is quite strong and will stain the print unevenly unless you keep it spread out with water.

Mix up a quantity of the colour on a palette or old saucer with plenty of water until you have the desired colour. It is better to make this too pale than too strong. Colour should be built up gradually, applying one thin layer over another. This way you can work up slowly to the right intensity of colour while maintaining maximum control. It is possible in this way to create colours that are intense without being crude.

Apply the inks with soft brushes of varying thicknesses depending on the area to be coloured. For very large areas, such as sky, it is advisable to apply the diluted ink with a pad of cotton wool, using a circular motion. This avoids the risk of brush marks and allows large areas to be covered quickly and evenly.

Glossy prints. It is rather more difficult to control the colour on a glossy print since it does not adhere to the surface well, so you must work with care. The addition of a very small amount of washing-up liquid to the ink may make its application easier.

Colouring part of a photograph. If you want just small areas of a print coloured it is possible to work on it dry. Observe the same rules regarding the strength of the ink. (Try out the colour

Courtesy of the Victoria and Albert Museum

on the white border of the print if the border is to be trimmed or covered up at a later stage.)

Oil-based method

Photo-tinting kits, consisting of a box of tubes of oil colour, pointed sticks for applying colour, reducing oil, turpentine and sizing fluid, such as Winsor and Newton's Photo Oil Colours, are obtainable at photographic shops and art materials suppliers.

Prepare the print by rubbing turpentine or sizing fluid into it with cotton wool (sizing fluid leaves a slightly oily shine). Then leave it to dry completely. Again, the colour is very concentrated so apply it sparingly. Mix the colour on your palette; the intensity of colour can be lessened with reducing oil and the paint made more runny with turpentine.

Apply the colour using one of the pointed sticks with a small piece of cotton wool wound round the point. After applying the colour, rub it in

This photograph was taken in the nineteenth century by Julia Cameron, one of the best-known photographers of her day. The picture was coloured by Barbara Firth using the oil-based method.

with cotton wool.

As in the ink process you should work up to the strongest colours.

You will need a small brush for the details instead of a stick.

The advantages of this method are that it is easy to get soft edges and, if you make a mistake, you can rub off the colour with cotton wool and turpentine. The disadvantage is that it is difficult to apply intense colour in small areas.

When you have finished colouring your photograph leave it to dry off completely.

Now you are ready to mount your photograph on card if you wish. (If you intend to put the picture into a frame, it may be advisable to leave it un-mounted as a mounted print could be too thick to fit into the frame.)

Previous chapters have described how to make traditional card and pleated paper lampshades. Another original aspect of lampshade making is to utilize today's materials and entirely different techniques to make hanging lampshades with a strikingly modern look. The lampshades illustrated here are made from paper cups and plates glued or fastened to each other and built up into interesting geometric shapes.

Using cups

Collect cups (whether of paper, plastic or polystyrene) which have been used for vending machine drinks or for a party. Wash and dry them carefully and store until you have a collection large enough to make a shade. Obviously, all the cups which go to make up one shade must be the same size and type.

The number of cups you will need and the size of the finished shade depend on the size and shape of cup used. These vary (fig.1). Tall, gently tapered

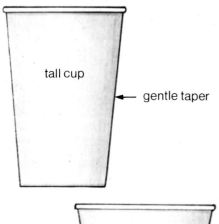

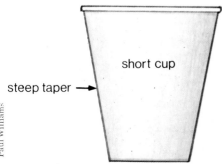

1. *Cups with a gentle taper will build up into a large shade; those with a steep taper will make a smaller shade.*

cups build into a spherical shape only very gradually; the round lampshade was made from short paper cups with a steep taper; the globe is considerably smaller than would be possible if tall, gently tapering cups were used. (If you wish, you can paint the cups before assembling them, but they will become more opaque.)

In order to make a perfect sphere, you must start with a single cup and make the whole shade by building up round it. (Making two separate halves or several sections and then trying to fit them together simply does not work.) Each cup is joined to its neighbour at the mouth and at the base. Staples can be used for joining the cups at the mouth, but the stapler is impractical for joining the bases. Glue can be used for this. It shows less than staples but, of course, takes longer to use. Only one or two cups at a time can be added to the shade and the glue must be left to dry according to the manufacturer's instructions. If you are using plastic cups, Sellotape will hold the cups together while the glue dries. Otherwise, large paper clips, clothes pegs or rubber bands can be used to hold the cups in position.

Always let the completed lampshade 'rest' for a day between completion and hanging. This is to ensure that no strain is put on it until it is thoroughly dry.

You will need:

Cups, all of the same size and material. An adhesive, such as Bostik 1, Evo-stik Clear, Durofix or UHU if you are using paper or hard plastic cups; or Bostik 12 (a polystyrene tile adhesive) or PVA if you are using polystyrene cups. Staples and stapler will have to be used with waxed paper cups.

Pegs, rubber bands or Sellotape to hold cups together while the glue is drying. An electric light fitting (with a low-watt bulb) which includes a flex. Lampshade ring (optional).

The spherical shade

Unless you have an enormous room and therefore want a really large shade, use stubby, sharply tapered cups. For a shade of about 50cm (20") diameter you will need about 120 cups.

☐ Begin by sticking three cups together and build the shade from there

(fig.2). Care must be taken not to let the rims of the cups overlap. Do not worry, however, if the cups do not all join at their bases. Leave a space at the bottom of the shade.

2. *The first stage in building up a sphere is to stick three cups together.*

☐ Make a hole in one of the cups at the top, through which you can insert the flex. Pull the flex right through the shade and out through the space at the bottom. Attach the bulb holder and bulb to the flex and slide the shade down until it rests on the bulb holder. If you wish to include a lampshade ring with the light fitting, this must be inserted when the shade is only half complete, and the rest of the shade built round it. Choose a dropped pendant fitting, which will help support the shade as well as hold the light bulb. Pull the flex through the shade, passing it through the small ring, and fit the bulb holder and bulb to the flex in the manner already described.

Glues

Since some glues contain ingredients which cause plastic to dissolve, it would be a pity if you found this out after completing the lampshade. Therefore test the suitability of the glue by sticking two or three cups together before embarking on the project. Use all glues sparingly.

Safety

As a precaution against the risk of fire, always use very low wattage bulbs with these types of lampshade. 60 watts should be the maximum. Be particularly careful if you are using polystyrene, as this type of plastic melts at only 75°C (167°F).

This spherical shade is made of short, steeply tapering cups. The wide tops of the cups mean that there are relatively wide gaps between them, allowing for plenty of light.

The domed shade

The domed shade is easier to make than the spherical one. For a shade about 60cm (24″) in diameter, you will need about 110 cups about 10cm (4″) high.

☐ Simply fix the first circle of cups together while resting them on a table (fig.3). Use about 26 cups. Wait till the glue is dry on the first layer before proceeding.

☐ Place the second row of cups above every other join and slightly behind the rims of the cups in the lower row (fig.4).

The domed shade is surprisingly easy to make. The pool of light it creates makes it suitable for hanging over a dining table, from a long flex.

☐ Continue in the same way for five rows (fig.5), then fill in the top. Some

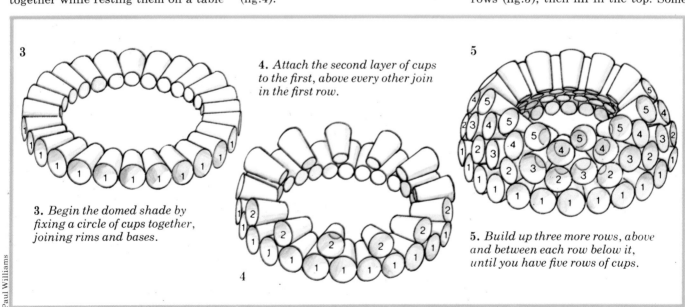

4. *Attach the second layer of cups to the first, above every other join in the first row.*

3. *Begin the domed shade by fixing a circle of cups together, joining rims and bases.*

5. *Build up three more rows, above and between each row below it, until you have five rows of cups.*

slight flexing of the rims of some of the cups may be necessary, in order to make them meet the adjoining rims.

The bulb and ring can be inserted easily from the open bottom of this completed shade.

Using plates

Disposable picnic plates can also be used for making a lampshade. They can be painted very successfully.

You will need:

About 20 paper plates.

Split paper fasteners.

Sharply pointed scissors.

☐ Begin by making two small holes with the points of the scissors in the opposite edges of each of eight plates which make up the bottom row.

☐ Fix them together with split paper fasteners to form a circle (fig.6). This

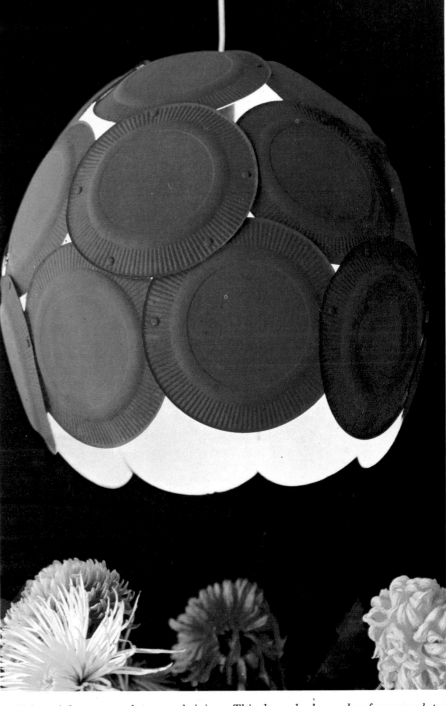

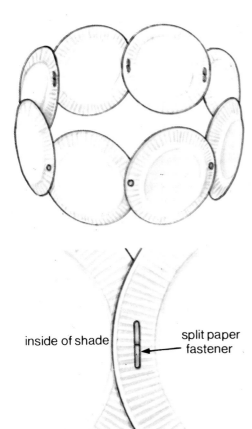

inside of shade — split paper fastener

6. *Begin the plate lampshade by fixing eight plates together with split paper fasteners, to form a circle. Make sure the fasteners fold back on the inside.*

method of holding them together is better than glue, as the plates must be curved to form a tulip shape. A long stapler could be used but this might be difficult; adhesive, if used, should be applied as described for the shades made with cups.

☐ Make another small hole in the top and slightly to one side of each of these eight plates.

☐ Take eight more plates and join them together in the same way as for the first eight plates, using split paper fasteners. These become the second row.

☐ To attach the second row to the first, make a hole in the bottom of each plate to align with the holes made in the top of the plates in the first row and attach with split paper fasteners. The plates in the second row should be centred over the joins in the plates of the first row, as in the photograph. If any of the plates jut out at any point, instead of being part of a smooth surface, fasten down with more split paper fasteners.

This lampshade made of paper plates has been painted very successfully. The edges of the plates at the bottom form a scalloped shape, making the shade resemble a tulip.

☐ Having made two rows, finish off with four plates at the top of the shade, joining them to the second row with split paper fasteners. Five gaps between the plates will occur round the top of the shade between these four plates and the second row, and at the top. The flex will pass through this top gap. These gaps should be equal in size if the plates are correctly joined.

Animal glove puppets

The antics of glove puppets have for centuries been a source of fascination, especially for children, and today puppet theatres are a traditional art form in many countries.

By adapting the basic head pattern of this glove puppet, various animals can be made and these could be used imaginatively in a theatrical production or simply as charming toys. The patterns given are for a cat's and rabbit's head but if you deepen the chin a little you will make a dog's head. If you make it shallower you will turn it into a lamb. However, the shape of the head is not as important when designing your own glove puppets as are the shape of the ears, eyes and mouth.

Suitable fabrics. Felt is perhaps the most suitable fabric for making glove puppets since it is easy to work with, comes in a wide range of colours and raw edges will not fray. Some pieces, such as the cat's facial markings shown here or the rabbit's paw pads, can be cut out and stuck or sewn on to the main body without the edges being turned under. When using other fabric, make sure you use a fabric that does not stretch or fray too easily such as printed cotton. Try to find a patterned fabric that is in some way related to the colours or markings on the animal.

Reducing the size. These glove puppets are made for a medium-sized adult hand. If they are to be used exclusively by small children, make the pattern a fraction smaller, by cutting off about 6mm ($\frac{1}{4}$″) all around the pieces. Make the puppets as described taking 6mm ($\frac{1}{4}$″) turnings where indicated.

The cat
You will need:
Tracing paper and pencil.

60cm x 60cm (24″x 24″) of black felt or patterned cotton fabric.

Scraps of white and coloured felt for the muzzle, nose and eyes.

A length of black wool for the mouth.

Kapok or synthetic stuffing for the head and tail.

4cm (1$\frac{1}{2}$″) length of 2.5cm (1″) diameter cardboard roll.

Sewing cotton and white button thread.

Fabric adhesive such as Copydex.

Beeswax or candlewax.

Melvin Grey

□ Trace pattern pieces overleaf and mark in the stitching lines, 6mm ($\frac{1}{4}$″) has been allowed on all seams. Label each piece with its name and the number to be cut out, mark the straight grain line.

□ Pin the pattern pieces to the felt or fabric placing on the fold where indicated.

□ For the black cat, use black felt for all the body pieces including the tail, outer ears and iris for the eye. Use white for eye whites and paws, muzzle and inner ears, and pink for the nose.

□ For a cat in cotton fabric cut out the body, head and tail in printed cotton, the paws, muzzle, eyes, outer and inner ears in coloured felt and the nose in black felt.

Body. With right sides facing, sew the two back body pieces together along the centre back seam.

□ Sew each felt paw piece to the corresponding front or back body overlapping by about 6mm ($\frac{1}{4}$″) and top stitching in position.

□ With right sides facing pin the front to the back matching the paws and side seams. Stitch all round, leaving the bottom and neck open.

□ Trim the seam allowance neatly, snipping at curves, and turn through to the right side.

Tail. With right sides facing, fold the tail in half lengthways. Stitch down the long edges and around the curved end, leaving the short straight end open. Trim and turn to right side.

□ Stuff the tail lightly and sew up the end.

□ Stitch the tail firmly to the body across the back seam and level with the back legs.

Head. With right sides facing, pin the centre gusset piece to the side head pieces, matching points A and B. Stitch gusset and chin seams leaving the neck edge open (fig.1). Trim and turn right side out.

□ Stuff the head well but do not stuff the neck.

□ Insert the cardboard roll into the neck, and add more stuffing where necessary to make the head firm.

□ To prevent the stuffing getting into the roll, cut a circle of felt a little larger than the diameter of the roll. Stick to the stuffing above the upper end of the roll (fig.2).

□ Insert the stiffened neck into the body opening, overlapping by about 2cm ($\frac{3}{4}$″) (fig.3) and slip stitch together.

□ If using cotton fabric first turn in the neck edge of the body all round and tack with double thread.

□ Stick the inner ears to the outer ears. Fold a dart in the centre of each ear, and pin ears to head.

□ Now pin the white felt muzzle shape, and the eyes in position so that you can adjust them if necessary to produce an

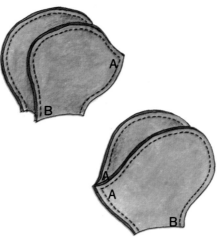

1. Head pieces sewn together.

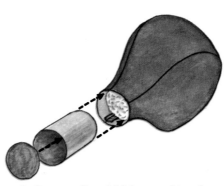

2. Insert roll; add felt to seal head.

3. Attaching stiffened neck into body.

4. Inner ear stitched to outer ear.

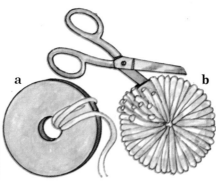

Barbara Firth

5. Making a wool pompon for tail.

a b

effective cat-like expression.

□ Sew on the ears and the muzzle using contrasting cotton and large stitches to achieve a furry effect.

□ Stick the black felt irises on to the eye whites then stick the assembled eyes to the head.

□ Stick on the pink nose piece, and use black wool to embroider the mouth.

□ Make whiskers by threading three 15cm (6″) lengths of white button thread to either side of the muzzle making a small stitch. Secure by knotting close to the muzzle—this makes six whiskers each side. (The whiskers can be stiffened with beeswax or candlewax.)

□ Sew three large black cotton stitches through each paw for claws.

Note: if you are using a cotton fabric, turn under and sew a small hem. Narrow elastic can be inserted into the hem so that the puppet fits neatly over the wrist.

The rabbit

You will need:

Tracing paper and pencil.
60cm x 60cm (24″x 24″) white felt.
15cm x 15cm (6″x 6″) pink felt for inner ears and paw pads.
18cm x 18cm (7″x 7″) blue felt for waistcoat.
Scraps of grey and black felt for eyes.
12cm (5″) red ribbon for a bow tie.
Scraps of black wool for the paws and the nose.
White wool for tail.
2 circles of card 5cm (2″) in diameter.

□ Cut out the same basic pattern pieces as for the cat but use the rabbit trace patterns for the ears, paws, pads and eyes. Use pink felt for the inner ears and the paw pads.

□ Make the rabbit body as for the cat.

□ Stitch pink inner ears to the outer white ears, so that the pink felt is taut while the white felt is loose and curved (fig.4). This leaves a hollow centre and will help to keep the ears upright.

□ After making and attaching the white paws, stick a pink paw on the front of each paw. Stitch black claws as for the cat. Stitch on the eyes.

□ Embroider the nose and mouth.

□ Make a pompon for a tail by winding white wool round two card circles with centre cut out (fig.5a). Snip the wool all round the outer edge (fig.5b), and secure firmly round the middle. Remove card and stitch pompon in place.

□ To make the simple felt waistcoat cut along the green lines marked on body pattern and cut out in blue felt.

□ Stitch the shoulder and side seams.

□ Slip the waistcoat on the rabbit. Turn back the corners at the neck and stitch down to form revers.

□ Use the length of red ribbon to make a bow tie and sew it in position under the chin to complete the rabbit.

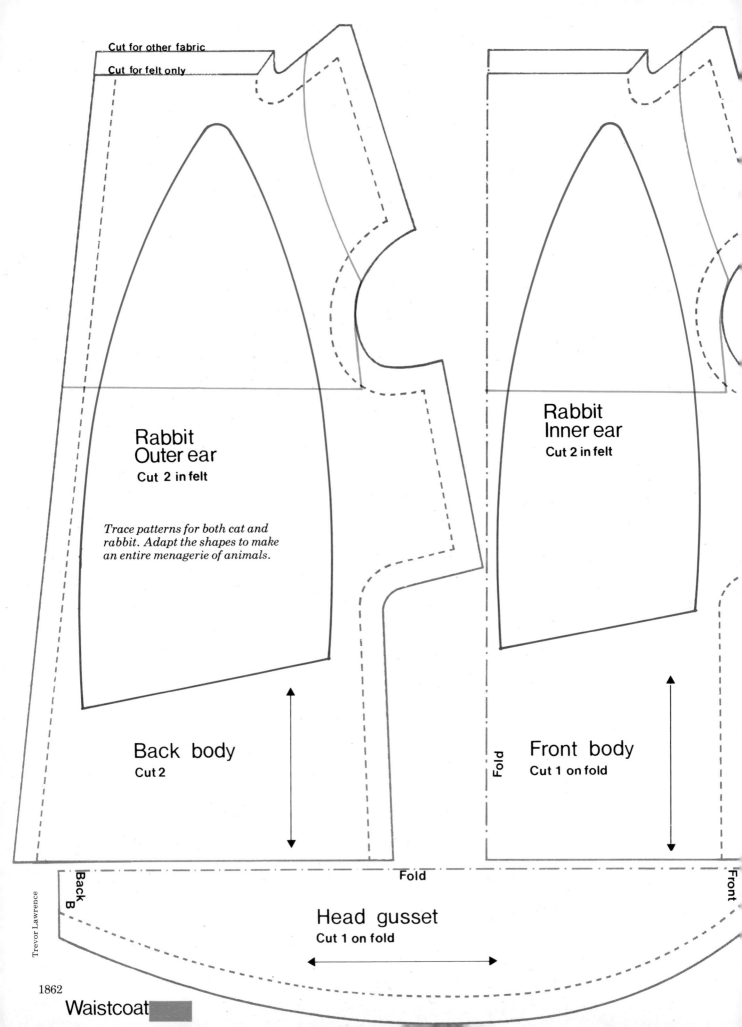

Cut for other fabric

Cut for felt only

Rabbit
Outer ear
Cut 2 in felt

Trace patterns for both cat and rabbit. Adapt the shapes to make an entire menagerie of animals.

Rabbit
Inner ear
Cut 2 in felt

Back body
Cut 2

Fold

Front body
Cut 1 on fold

Back B

Fold

Front

Trevor Lawrence

1862

Waistcoat

Head gusset
Cut 1 on fold

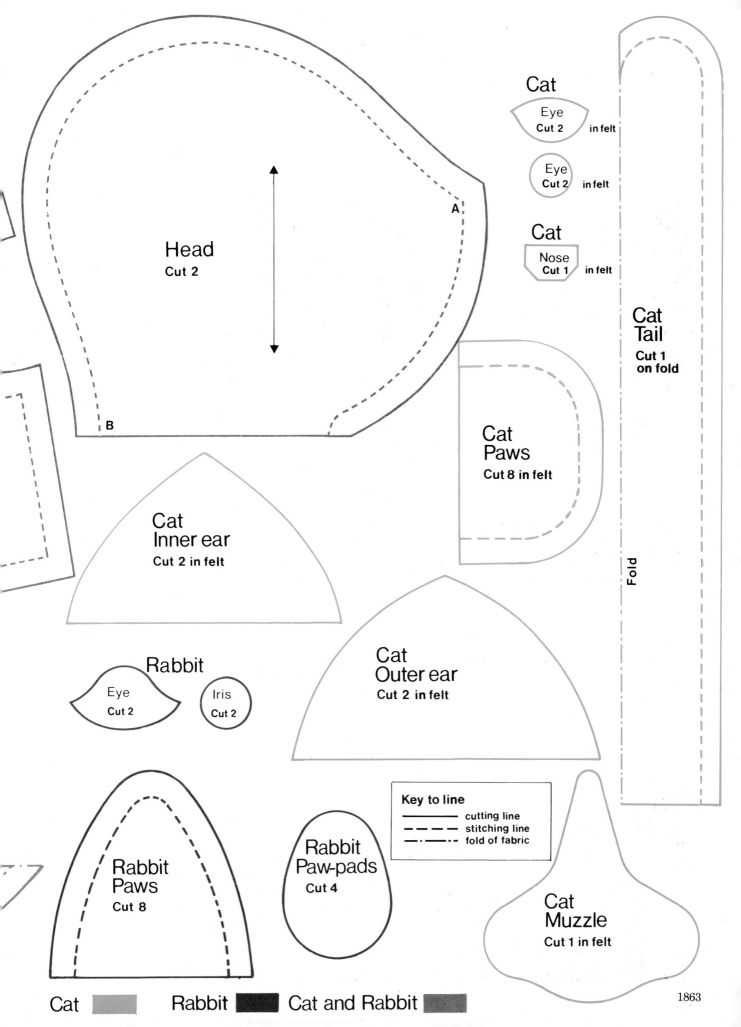

Cat
Eye
Cut 2 in felt

Eye
Cut 2 in felt

Cat
Nose
Cut 1 in felt

Cat
Tail
Cut 1
on fold

Head
Cut 2

A

B

Cat
Paws
Cut 8 in felt

Fold

Cat
Inner ear
Cut 2 in felt

Rabbit
Eye
Cut 2

Iris
Cut 2

Cat
Outer ear
Cut 2 in felt

Key to line
——— cutting line
- - - stitching line
—·—·— fold of fabric

Rabbit
Paws
Cut 8

Rabbit
Paw-pads
Cut 4

Cat
Muzzle
Cut 1 in felt

Cat   Rabbit   Cat and Rabbit

1863

How to repair veneer surfaces

Many wooden articles that would once have been made of hardwoods such as mahogany or teak are now built from cheap softwoods and covered with a decorative hardwood veneer to simulate a hardwood finish.

Comparatively speaking, veneered furniture is frail and easily damaged. Common causes of damage include cigarette or hot plate burns, knocks from children playing, and loose pieces of veneer getting caught on clothing and tearing away from the surface. All these produce minor local damage which can be repaired by patching.

Making a new piece to match the old veneer is sometimes a problem but it is easier than the alternative which is to re-veneer the whole article. There are also various techniques which help to conceal the join between old and new.

Many DIY stores and timber merchants sell veneer in a wide range of woods so there should be little difficulty in getting the type you need. The problem is that most dealers will insist on selling a whole sheet of veneer. This usually measures about 92cm x 45cm ($3' \times 1\frac{1}{2}'$). There are, however, certain stores which deal in small pieces.

Nearly all veneer is of the same thickness—about 2mm ($\frac{1}{16}''$)—although there are some exceptions. One of these is the veneer border around the leather tops of some desks and tables where the veneer has to be the same thickness as the leather. This may be as much as 3mm ($\frac{1}{8}''$), in which case a veneer would have to be specially ordered.

If you cannot get veneer exactly the same colour as the piece you are patching, buy a lighter colour as it can always be darkened by staining. In any case, the veneer usually darkens when polished.

Handle veneer carefully, particularly in large sheets, as it splits very easily.

You will need:

Tracing paper, carbon paper, pencil.
Steel ruler or straight edge.
Trimming knife.
Narrow chisel.
White woodworking adhesive or, for large or difficult patches, Scotch glue.
G-clamps and some blocks of scrap wood.
Brown paper.
An electric iron.
Very fine grade and flour grade glass-paper and wood block.
Cabinet scraper—a flat, rectangular piece of metal used mainly for removing old varnish and lacquer.
Proprietary wood filler—optional.
Ready-mixed spirit-based wood stain.
Warrington or veneer hammer.
Very fine wire wool and teak oil.

An example of veneered furniture. Note the damaged edge in need of repair.

Bill McLaughlin

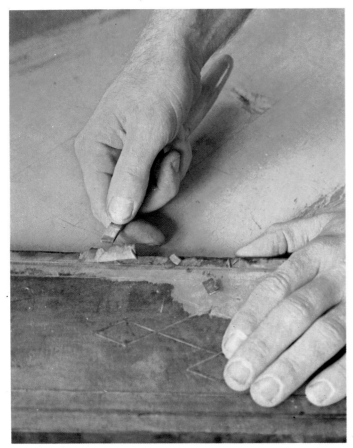

1. *Use chisel bevel side up at edge of damaged strip.*

2. *Place strip of veneer on damaged area and cut to fit.*

Nelson Hargreaves

Cutting edge patches

Most damage to veneered furniture is to the edge of the surface but, fortunately, this is also the easiest part to repair invisibly.

Wherever possible, repair a damaged edge by removing and replacing a straight strip running along the whole edge of the piece with the grain of the veneer. In this way the old and new pieces will be joined along the line of their grain, thus concealing the join. The join will also be a straight line which makes it fairly easy to fit.

☐ First remove the polish around the damaged area with a cabinet scraper in order to discover the natural colour of the wood.

☐ Match a piece of the new veneer to the old wood. A quick way of seeing whether the new piece will match when polished is to wet it. The colour of the wet wood is an indication of what it will look like when polished.

Note: if this method is used, wet both sides of the new veneer in order to prevent warping.

☐ Using the chisel remove the damaged area of veneer. Hold the chisel, bevel side up, at the edge and bevel side down further in (fig.1).

☐ Cut the new veneer to fit using a ruler and trimming knife (fig.2).

Delicate veneers should be dampened on both sides before cutting as this helps prevent splitting.

As the edges of the object are the most vulnerable the new piece should be stuck on with a strong glue such as Scotch glue as described further on.

☐ Once the glue has set, the new veneer can be trimmed on the outer edges with a very sharp chisel or trimming knife.

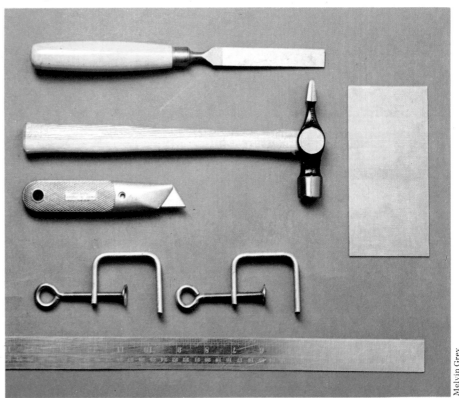

Tools—the cross pein hammer is used to press out air bubbles.

Melvin Grey

Cutting patches

Knotty veneer, ie veneer in which the natural patterns of the wood have been used, and veneer damaged in the middle of a surface are best repaired by replacing the damaged section with a boat-shaped patch, ie an oval shape with pointed ends. The long diameter of the oval points along the general direction of the grain, will subtly blend into the overall surface.

Determining the size. Find the most suitable size for the patch by putting a piece of tracing paper over the damaged area and drawing 'boat' shapes on it until you find one that seems right (fig.3). Remember that the pointed ends must run with the grain; the more a join runs across the grain the more it will show, so keep the ends of the oval as pointed as possible. Once you have found a suitable size, draw a

few lines along it to show the direction of the grain.

☐ Use a piece of carbon paper to transfer the shape to the new veneer. Press very lightly and get the grain running the right way by means of the lines on the tracing.

Cutting the patch. With the trimming knife cut out the shape. The handle of the blade should slope outwards at an angle of 45° so that the cut edge slants. It is a good idea to cut out the shape slightly too large as this will give you a chance to move it around over the damaged section to match the grain more exactly.

When cutting a straight strip of veneer it is not necessary to slope the knife.

☐ When the correct position has been found, hold the piece firmly in place and draw around it lightly with a sharp pencil.

A wooden box showing the fine finish which can be achieved with veneer.

☐ Remove the patch and cut around the mark on the surface of the damaged section, just inside the pencil line, and holding the knife at the same 45° angle used for cutting out the patch. Be careful not to cut too much of the old veneer. If the patch is too big you can cut it down but if it is too small you will have to make a new patch. The slanting join serves to hide any small discrepancies.

☐ Remove the damaged veneer inside the cut line with a very sharp, narrow chisel held bevel side down. You should just chisel out the old veneer and the glue under it, without gouging the wood to which the veneer is glued. Large areas of glue can be removed by first wetting the old glue slightly with hot water—but do this carefully.

☐ Try the patch in the hole and trim where necessary. It is now ready for gluing.

Gluing patches. Patches need to be glued in very strongly and held in place until the glue has set. Normally white woodworking adhesive is suitable but for large, difficult patches and edge patches use Scotch glue. The white adhesive can be used without clamps if necessary but, wherever possible, use clamps.

To hold the patch firmly in place use a G-clamp with a wood block underneath it. The block should cover the whole patch or the edges will curl. A good improvised clamp for a horizontal surface would be a sheet of glass with three or four bricks laid on top.

☐ Apply the glue, thinly but evenly, to the two surfaces and press the patch into place.

☐ Air bubbles are forced out by rubbing the new veneer lightly with a Warrington or veneer hammer.

☐ Wipe off any glue that oozes out with a damp cloth.

☐ Put a sheet of brown paper over the patch to absorb the surplus glue, apply the clamp and wood block, and leave as long as required.

☐ A patch glued with the woodworking adhesive can be ironed in place with an electric iron set to 'warm'. When the adhesive is tacky, cover the patch with brown paper and run the iron back and forth until the glue is dry—this will take about 20 minutes.

(If you do not have an iron or any clamps, you can use impact adhesive, preferably the thixotropic kind which allows you to slide the patch about. However, the repair will not last for very long.)

Finish

When the glue is thoroughly dry, pull off as much of the brown paper as possible—carefully wetting the paper helps.

☐ Then wrap some very fine glasspaper around a flat-surfaced wood block and sand off all remaining traces of paper and glue. Continue sanding until the surface of the patch is level with the veneer around it. Always sand along the grain, finishing with flour grade glasspaper (the finest), so that the surface is completely smooth.

☐ If your surface is very light coloured or has a coarse, open grain—such as oak, ash, rosewood and sapele—seal it with a proprietary grain filler in the appropriate colour. This prevents large amounts of polish sinking into the wood, discolouring it and making it hard to achieve a good sheen.

☐ Rub the filler into the veneer and smooth it with the flour grade paper.

French polishing. Before applying

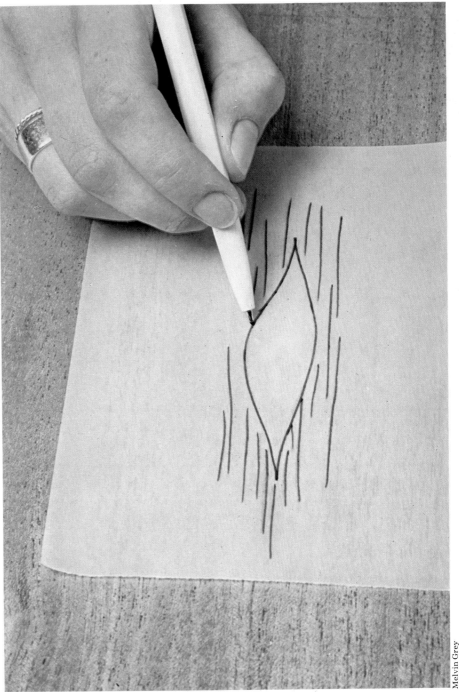

Melvin Grey

any french polish to the patch (Wood Finishes chapter 5, page 1726) make sure it will turn the right colour when polished.

As a rough guide, look at the area immediately around the patch where the old polish has been sanded off. If it is not the same colour as the patch, you will need to stain the patch to match.

Staining the patch. To stain the patch use a ready-mixed spirit-based wood stain. The depth of its colour does not matter because you can dilute the polish with methylated spirit. What does matter is the tone—ie whether it is, for example, reddish or yellowish.

☐ Experiment to find the right dilution on offcuts of veneer then paint the

3. Place a piece of tracing paper over the damaged section and mark out a pointed oval. Mark in lines of grain.

diluted mix on to the patch.

Note: a water-based wood dye is not suitable because it spreads out on application.

Satin finishes. Some modern furniture has a satin finish. This is achieved by painting the veneer with a 50/50 mixture of clear polyurethane varnish and white spirit. Allow to dry, sand with a very fine grade glasspaper and apply another coat. Always paint along the grain to avoid leaving brush marks. Finish by rubbing with very fine wire wool and a little teak oil. This finish is specially suited for teak veneers.

Egyptian wall hanging

Every aspect of existence that the occupant hoped to enjoy in the afterlife was recorded in the tombs of the Egyptian pharaohs. Here the preparations for a feast have inspired an appliqué wall hanging. The angular silhouettes are ideal for interpretation in this medium. To keep the primitive feeling use coarse fabrics such as linen or hessian for the background and finer cotton, which could be dyed with cold-

Trevor Lawrence

Chris Lewis

water dyes or natural plant dyes, for the figures. Apply the design with turned-under edges (see Appliqué chapter 2, page 350) hemmed with embroidery thread and add more embroidery for the details. The finished size is 120cm x 38cm (47″ x 15″).

Below: sketches of some of the motifs, used repeatedly in the wall hanging can be templates used as appliqué patterns.

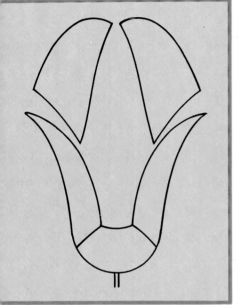

Egyptian-style hanging in soft, muted colours combines appliqué and embroidery. The detail (above) shows successful primitive effect of simple stitching.

Deep buttoning on foam

Cloth — upholstery 11

Deep buttoning is a decorative form of upholstery. It developed during the 19th century from the need to hold loose padding materials (horsehair and fibre) in place on vertical surfaces such as the backs of chairs and settees.

The cover fabric is pulled down deep into the padding at regular intervals over the surface and secured with buttons which are tied on with twine. The padding is enclosed in the pockets thus formed.

The process causes a puckering of the fabric between the buttons which is neatened by folding the fabric into pleats. The pleats stay in place most easily when they lie on the bias grain of the fabric, so the most usual pattern of buttoning is based on a diamond shape.

For deep buttoning to look really good, the fabric must be smooth and taut with little puckering, and the mounds of padding between the buttons must be even in size and well rounded. This takes considerable skill when working with a loose padding material but is much easier with foam rubber—although in this case the technique is used for a purely decorative effect.

This chapter describes how to work deep buttoning with foam padding on a solid wood foundation such as for a headboard—this is the easiest project to attempt while gaining practice in handling the fabric. A later chapter shows how to develop the technique for traditional upholstery.

Deep-buttoned headboard

The techniques described here could also be used for a stool made with a solid wood foundation rather than an open frame.

The foundation. This may be an old wooden headboard (these can often be bought cheaply from a junk shop) or it could be a new headboard cut from 13mm ($\frac{1}{2}$") chipboard or plywood. It may have curved edges but it should not be an intricate shape because you will not be able to achieve a smooth outline. If you do have an intricate shape it would be better to inset the padding leaving a border of wood around the edge, as described in Upholstery chapter 5, page 748.

Making templates

☐ If the headboard is fitted to the bed with struts put it in position on the bed (if it is not already there) and mark the height of the mattress. Remove the headboard, place it on a large sheet of paper and draw round the edge of the wood. Cut out along the lines.

Deep buttoning with foam padding on a wooden foundation makes a luxurious bedhead and is a good introduction to this traditional technique.

Mark the height of the mattress on the paper and draw a line across it. Cut along this line. This template is the area of the board which will be padded and deep-buttoned. The area below will simply be covered with fabric and the mattress will fit up against it.

The buttoning pattern. To plan the positions of the buttons, mark the centre of each edge of the padding template. Draw lines across the template between the centre points on opposite edges.

☐ Working outwards from these lines, draw a grid with parallel vertical lines about 10cm (4") apart and horizontal lines 15cm (6") apart. Draw diagonal lines through the intersections to form diamonds of the required size. Mark the positions of the buttons at the angles of the diamonds. Leave a clear border without buttons of at least 5cm (2") all round the edge.

Fabric template. On a second piece of paper, about one and a half times the size of the padding template, make a pattern for the fabric by drawing a grid with the same number of lines but spaced 3cm ($1\frac{1}{4}$") further apart than on the padding template to allow for the fabric being pulled down into the padding. Mark on the button positions as for the padding template.

☐ Working from the outside lines of the grid, mark the area of the un-buttoned area to correspond with that on the padding template. Then mark a second line, a minimum of 5cm (2") from this, to give a margin for turnings. Cut along this second line.

Fabrics

Cover fabric. Choose a fabric which will not show the dirt quickly and which can be sponged or dry-cleaned easily—a Dralon velvet is ideal. Avoid patterned fabrics because you will have trouble in matching it at joins. To calculate the amount of fabric needed, measure the width of the fabric template. If this width is less than the width of the fabric you intend to use—as it will be for a small single bed with fabrics of 122cm (48") or more—allow an amount of fabric of the height of the template plus a piece 10cm (4") deeper than the mattress.

If the width is more than the fabric, you will have to allow twice the height of the template plus the piece 10cm (4") deeper than the mattress, so that you can join sections to make up the width. Ideally, this joining on the padded section should not be done with a normal seam but by a special technique known as 'vandyking' during the buttoning process. This is described later in the chapter.

Calico. Allow enough calico to make 10cm (4") wide strips to fit the perimeter of the padding.

Covering the board
You will need:
Wooden foundation.
Cover fabric.
Calico.
Templates.
Foam, 7.5cm (3") thick and 1.5cm ($\frac{1}{2}$") larger all round than padding template.
Button moulds with 1.5cm ($\frac{1}{2}$") diameter (it is wise to buy one or two more than the basic number required in case you lose one). When you need a large number of buttons it is often worth having the buttons covered professionally.
One 15mm ($\frac{1}{2}$") improved tack for each button.
Tack hammer.
Several 1cm ($\frac{3}{8}$") fine tacks.
Staple gun (optional) and staples.
Twine. Use nylon twine rather than traditional upholsterer's twine to give extra strength.
Clear adhesive such as Bostik I.
Drill and 3mm ($\frac{1}{8}$") wood drill bit.
Upholstery needle, 20cm (8") long.
Regulator.
Ruler, tailor's chalk.
Needle and thread (optional).

☐ Transfer the markings of the button positions from the padding template to the headboard. Drill a hole through the wood at each position.

☐ Place a temporary improved tack below each hole on the back of the headboard (fig.1).

☐ Cut or tear 10cm (4") wide strips of

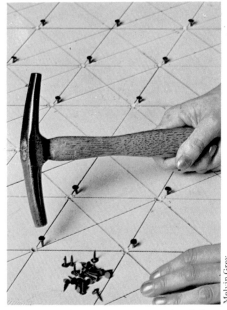

Melvin Grey

1. *Hammering temporary tacks below the holes on the back of the board.*

calico to fit the perimeter of the foam as described for the plain padded headboard in Upholstery chapter 5, page 748.

☐ Stick on the calico strips and attach the foam to the wood as described in the same chapter.

Main cover. Cut out the fabric using

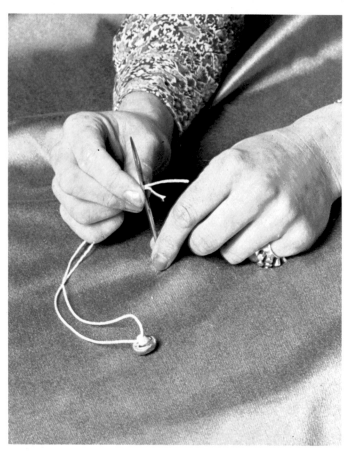

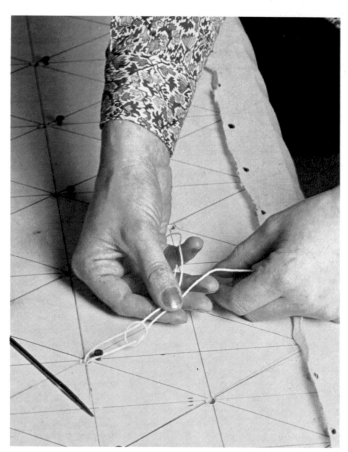

2. *Threading the needle with both ends of twine before pulling the needle through to the back of the board.*

3. *Tightening the slip knot round the tack to pull down the button on the foam on the right side of the board.*

4. *Using the flat end of a regulator to neaten into pleats the fullness that forms between the buttons.*

5. *Folding the fullness at the edges of the board into pleats which lie at right angles to the edge.*

the fabric template. If you are going to join the fabric by vandyking, read the section on this technique before you begin. If you prefer to use a plain seam, work this before beginning the buttoning by attaching two equal strips to the sides of a main panel and making plain seams with 1.5cm ($\frac{1}{2}$") turnings.

□ For the unpadded section at the bottom of the board, cut a rectangle of fabric of the required size plus 10cm (4") each way for turnings.

□ From the remaining fabric cover the required number of button moulds.

□ Using the fabric template, mark the button positions on the fabric with either tailor's chalk or tailor's tacks.

□ Place the fabric on the foam so that the centre button positions are aligned.

□ Working on the centre diamond and starting on the back of the board, pass the needle eye first through the hole in the wood and out through the foam and fabric. Check that the needle is straight and leave it with about 5cm (2") protruding. Thread about 50cm (20") twine through the shank of the button and then thread both ends of the twine through the eye of the needle (fig.2). Pull the needle back through the board, unthread it and tie the twine in a slip knot below the tack (fig.3). Tighten the knot and leave the ends hanging.

□ Repeat this process for the remaining buttons of the centre diamond, using the flat end of the regulator to neaten the fullness that forms between the buttons into pleats (fig.4). The exposed folds of pleats should face downwards.

□ Continue working from the centre diamond outwards in this way, forming one complete diamond at a time. It is usually easiest to set the pleats and to keep the grain of fabric straight if you form each diamond before tightening the twine.

□ When all the button positions are formed, neaten the fullness at the edges into pleats which lie at right angles to the edge so they face outwards from the centre top and downwards on the sides (fig.5).

□ Smooth the edges of the fabric round to the back of the headboard at the top and sides. Be careful not to pull too tightly or you may lose the outside pleats. Where you have left an unpadded section at the foot of the headboard tack the bottom edge through the single thickness close to the bottom of the foam on front of headboard.

□ Tighten all the slip knots again and hammer down the tacks.

□ Cover the unpadded section at the bottom of the headboard as described in Upholstery chapter 5. If you wish to cover the back of the headboard, place a piece of upholstery wadding over it and then follow the method described in the same chapter.

Vandyking

In this method of joining the fabric for the padded section no sewing is actually done because the fabric is cut in a zigzag shape so that the edges of the join can be concealed under the pleats of the diamonds. The fabric is held in place by the button twine.

□ Start buttoning with a full fabric width, working from the middle of

□ Mark the button pattern on the new panel of fabric and lay it in place on the part still to be covered on one side of the headboard so that the grain of the fabric is absolutely square and the edge overlaps by 3cm (1"). Cut along this edge in a zigzag pattern to correspond with the first edge and clip into the angles for 1.5cm ($\frac{1}{2}$") (fig.6).

□ Fold under the edges for 1.5cm

the headboard out to the sides as previously described. When you reach the last row of buttons possible with the width, form all the pleats but do not tighten the twine. Trim off the excess fabric at the sides to within 1.5cm ($\frac{1}{2}$") of the pleats, following the zigzag line of the diamond shape. Leaving the pleats formed, remove the last row of buttons.

($\frac{1}{2}$") on the sides which come at the top of each diamond on the second panel (fig.7). Lay these *over* the top edge of the last diamonds formed in the main panel, so that the folds are quite level. Tuck the edges which come at the bottom of the diamonds on the new piece *under* the folds at the bottoms of those in the main panel (see fig.6). Stitch down with twine in the normal way.

Melvin Grey

Silver wire jewellery

Gold and silver can be joined by soldering and once you have familiarized yourself with the soldering techniques, using scrap wire or tin cans (Metal chapter 18, page 1388), you can try your hand at simple silver jewelry. These articles are made from silver wire, cut and shaped into links which are soldered together. Care must be taken during the actual soldering to ensure that the joins are not too noticeable.

Wire

Gold and silver wire are obtainable from silver and goldsmiths and are sold by weight, length and thickness (gauge—see Metal chapter 3, page 127). Although round wire is used for the jewelry described here, square wire is also available. It is more expensive as it is heavier.

You should begin working with silver wire as it is cheaper than gold.

Silver necklace

This silver necklace is made from round silver wire. It consists of three basic shapes of link: round, oval and square and is about 75cm (30″) long. The chain does not need a fastening clasp as it is long enough to go over one's head.

You will need: 215cm (86″) of 1.6mm (gauge 14-16) silver wire.

A slightly domed hammer and a steel block to use as an anvil.

15cm (6″) length of round wood dowel, 10mm (⅜″) in diameter.

15cm (6″) length of 10mm (⅜″) square wood dowel or beading.

Wooden ruler about 2.5cm (1″) wide.

Piercing saw, fine metal file and tin snips.

Asbestos mat.

Tweezers and a fine brush

Alum.

Medium solder and an acid flux eg borax flux.

Fine emery paper, tripoli polish, jeweller's rouge and a fine cloth.

Household detergent and an old toothbrush.

Soldering tools and equipment—see Metal chapter 15, page 1130.

Annealing or tempering makes the wire soft and pliable so that it can be bent easily. Wind the wire into a coil about 5cm (3″) in diameter. Tuck the ends in securely to stop it unwinding. With the blowtorch heat the wire all over, taking care to move the flame steadily around the circle of wire as too much heat in one place might melt or distort the metal.

☐ When the wire is a dull red colour, remove the flame and cool the wire in water.

The links. Take 60cm (24″) of the tempered wire and wind it tightly around the piece of square dowel as near to the end of the wood as you can.

Matching silver wire jewelry designed by Gill Dutfield.

Sandra Lousada

□ With a piercing saw cut through the wire, pushing the coil to the end as each link is separated (fig.1).

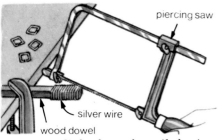

1. *Cutting links from the coiled wire.*

Repeat this with 80cm (32″) of wire wound around the round wooden dowel and with 75cm (30″) around the ruler. You will need 12 square, 12 oval and 24 round links.

Soldering. The square and oval links must now be soldered separately to make them whole. The round links are not soldered till later.

□ With the metal file, file the cut edges of the link flat so that they fit together snugly. Solder will not 'jump' or fill gaps caused by rough edges.

□ Cut the medium solder into very small pieces by cutting down the strip with tin snips then cutting across as finely as possible (fig.2).

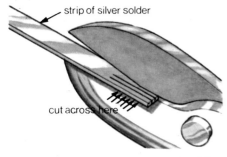

2. *Use tin snips to cut pieces of solder.*

□ Place several links on the asbestos and heat gently with the blowtorch. Using a fine brush, drop a little borax flux on each join. The metal should be just hot enough to make the borax splutter.

□ Pick up a piece of solder with the tweezers and place it on the join. Repeat the procedure with the other links.

□ Heat with the blowtorch until it is red hot and the solder melts. Remove the flame immediately and move on to the other links.

□ Make up an alum mixture of one level teaspoon of alum (bought from a chemist) and half a pint of water. Drop the soldered links into the mixture to remove the flux. This is called a 'pickle' and is used to remove the hardened borax from the silver after soldering.

□ Finally, remove any excess solder with a fine file.

Hammering. Place one of the soldered links on a steel block—you can use a large, flat pebble or the underside of an old iron held in a vice—and hammer gently, moving it around so that it thins evenly.

□ Turn the link over and hammer the other side, just enough to give it a beaten surface texture.

Do not hit too hard as this will make the link too thin.

Repeat the procedure with all the oval and square links.

The round links are now attached. They go between each square and oval link and great care must be taken when soldering these to ensure that they do not get soldered to the others.

□ Thread a square and an oval link on to a round link. Hold together the ones not to be soldered and place on the asbestos pad. Keep the round link join as far to the opposite side of the other two as possible, and solder (fig.3).

solder here

3. *Soldering the round link.*

Join all the links in this way until the chain is complete.

□ The round links must now be hammered to match the others. This must be done carefully by holding the square and oval ones on either side in your fingers and extending half the round one over the edge of the flat surface, hammering and moving it round continuously. The chain is then ready for polishing.

Polishing. If you want a very high polish, start by rubbing the article with a fine emery paper, then polish with tripoli on a soft cloth. Finish off with jeweller's rouge.

□ Should you want to retain the beaten surface appearance of the silver, use only the Tripoli and jeweller's rouge. If, however, parts of the link which have been filed look scratched then first smooth out the scratches with emery paper.

□ Wash the whole chain in detergent, scrubbing gently with an old toothbrush to clean off excess polish, and dry on a towel.

Bracelet

The bracelet is made in exactly the same way as the chain but without square links. Use round dowelling of 10mm ($\frac{3}{8}$″) and 12mm ($\frac{1}{2}$″) diameter to shape the links. You need 83cm (33″) of 1.6mm (gauge 14-16) silver wire to make nine large links and nine small. Anneal, solder, hammer and polish as with the necklace so that the links are joined in alternate sizes and make a complete circle. Again, there is no fastening catch as the bracelet is just big enough to slide over the hand.

Ear-rings

The ear-rings are made with similar links to the bracelet but a larger dowel, 16mm ($\frac{5}{8}$″) diameter, is used with the 12mm ($\frac{1}{2}$″) diameter dowel.

Four main links are made from 30cm (12″) of 1.6mm (gauge 14-16) silver wire. These are joined with jump rings made from about 10cm (4″) of .9mm (gauge 19-20) wire.

Alternatively, jump rings (see Metal chapter 1, page 25) can be bought from jeweller's supply shops but are costly.

□ Anneal the wire and make two links of each size, solder and hammer separately until flat.

□ You will need six jump rings. To make these wind the thin wire around a No.9 (US 5) knitting needle and cut to form a link. Do not hammer these.

□ Put one jump ring around each link and link them together so that the smaller of the hammered links sits inside the larger (fig.4).

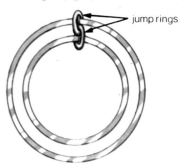

jump rings

4. *Link the ear-rings with jump rings.*

□ Now solder the jump rings. Great care must be taken when soldering as the joins are so close to the other links.

□ Use very small pieces of solder, keeping in mind that as the jump rings are so much smaller than the other links, they will melt sooner. Remove the flame immediately the solder flows or the rings will melt.

□ Put another jump ring on the outside of the ear-ring and through the top jump ring, then solder.

□ Polish both ear-rings and decide on which fittings you want. You can use either hooks or wire, or wires with butterfly backs, which are suitable for pierced ears. If screw fastenings are used, they will have to be linked to the jump ring before the jump ring is soldered. These findings are available from jewelry supply shops.

Adhesives for paper and card

You may want to mount a picture or design on to card or stiff paper before framing it or simply to reinforce it. In this chapter the various adhesives that can be used for mounting are discussed and instructions are given for mounting a picture on to card.

Adhesives

A number of different adhesives, available in most large art shops, can be used for mounting pictures on to a foundation such as card or stiff paper.

Rubber-based adhesives such as Cow Gum or Gloy Studio Gum must be applied to both surfaces to be stuck together.

☐ Spread a thin layer of adhesive over both surfaces to be joined together and leave until tacky—for about 10 to 15 minutes.

☐ Place a sheet of tissue paper over the glued area on the foundation leaving a strip about 6mm ($\frac{1}{4}$″) wide of glued area uncovered along the top.

☐ Place the picture over the tissue paper with the top of the picture over the uncovered strip of glue.

☐ Carefully line up the top of the picture with the top of the glued area on the foundation and press down.

☐ Gradually slide the piece of tissue paper out from between the picture and the foundation and, as you do so, smooth the two glued surfaces together, making sure there are no air bubbles trapped between the picture and the card.

☐ If you think you may want to re-position the picture, put the two surfaces together while the glue is still wet. If you wait until the glue is tacky before joining the two surfaces re-positioning will not be so easy.

☐ To remove any unwanted smears of glue, wait until they are dry and rub with an eraser.

Spray-on adhesive, such as Scotch Spray Mount adhesive, comes in aerosol cans, it is quick and easy to use and is particularly useful for mounting photographs.

☐ Spray the adhesive all over the back of the picture to be mounted.

☐ Position the picture on to the foundation and press down.

The picture can be lifted easily and re-positioned if the first attempt was not successful.

☐ Remove smears of glue with an eraser or a few drops of petroleum spirit on a rag (small cans of petroleum spirit such as Ronsonol, are sold in art shops as solvents).

Always use aerosol adhesive in a well-ventilated room as the fumes may be harmful if inhaled.

Victoria Drew

Double-sided tape. This is similar to ordinary transparent adhesive tape but is sticky on both sides. It comes in reels and is available in widths of up to 30cm (12″). To make the tape easy to use, one side is covered with protective paper.

☐ Stick strips of tape on the back of the picture to be mounted—strips along the top and bottom edge or along all four edges will be sufficient. Make sure you stick the tape right up to the edges of the picture for a neat finish.

☐ Remove the protective paper from the other side of the tape.

☐ Place the picture on to the foundation and smooth down.

This tape is clean and easy to use, but once the picture has been stuck it is impossible to re-position so you must be right the first time.

Double-sided tape is not suitable for mounting very thin paper as it tends to make the paper bubble and wrinkle.

Dry mounting tissue is sold in sheets looking rather like tissue paper.

☐ Cut a sheet of dry mounting tissue to the size of the picture to be mounted.

☐ Place the picture on the card and insert the dry mounting tissue between the picture and the card, aligning the edges of the dry mount and the picture.

☐ Place a thin sheet of paper over the three layers for protection and run a warm iron over the top.

☐ The warmth of the iron will activate the adhesive in the dry mounting tissue and stick the picture to the card.

Mounting a picture
You will need:

A sharp knife such as a Swann-Morton scalpel for cutting the card or paper.

A steel rule for measuring and for running the knife along when cutting straight lines.

A set square for measuring right-angled corners.

A pencil and eraser.

Adhesive (Cow Gum, Spray Mount, double-sided tape or dry mounting tissue).

☐ Make sure the corners of the picture to be mounted are square. If not, trim where necessary. Straight edges and right-angled corners are essential if the result is to look professional.

☐ Select the foundation. If the drawing is on semi-transparent paper, the colour of the foundation may show through, so choose carefully. If you want to leave a border round the edge of the picture choose a foundation of a colour that will suit the picture.

☐ Do not cut the foundation to size until after you have mounted the drawing.

☐ If you are using an adhesive that is spread on both surfaces, lightly mark in pencil the area of the foundation to be glued.

☐ Use adhesive, tape or dry mounting tissue as described earlier.

☐ When the picture has been stuck to the foundation, trim the foundation to size, leaving a border if desired, using the ruler, sharp knife and set square to obtain clean, right-angled corners.

Creative ideas 67

Printing ideas

Printing is fun—so don't wait for the next rainy day to try it. The techniques vary and many need little preparation.

The kitchen shown here has been given a 'face lift' with a combination of silk-screen printing and stencilling techniques. For extra appeal a single theme has been chosen and applied on

Below: try relief printing with fruits and vegetables.

everything, from the blinds to the egg-cup cover.

However, if you feel reluctant to attempt these more sophisticated techniques start by printing the simple tablecloth. The results will soon encourage you. The design here has been relief printed with leaves, but sections of fruit and vegetables could easily be substituted. Children, too, can participate.

For details and instructions on the methods shown see Printing chapter 1, page 76; chapter 13, page 962; chapter 14, page 1000; chapter 15, page 1028; chapter 16, page 1052 and Stencils chapter 3, page 270.

Above: bring a new look into your kitchen.

Below: close-up of simply printed tablecloth.

100 Ideés de Marie Claire/Philippe Capurro

Musical instruments: ocarinas

The ocarina, or globular flute, is an instrument of great antiquity and can be defined as an egg-shaped wind instrument made from clay or metal. The name comes from the Italian *oca*, meaning goose.

Historically, ocarinas have a world-wide distribution from the stone age onwards, occurring in various forms and at various levels of sophistication. The mellow notes of the 'little goose' have probably been heard at one time or another throughout Africa, Central and Southern America—and were certainly known to the Maya of Southern Mexico.

Inevitably, the ocarina was developed in more recent times in an attempt to bring it up to orchestral standards. The sophisticated version can have nine or ten holes, keys and tuning slides, and a compass of more than an octave.

However, the 'primitive' type can still be found, especially in Italy, as a carnival whistle in the form of a bird. Sometimes a couple of finger holes are provided for making fragments of a melody.

Two types of simple ocarina can be made from clay. The first has a large, open blowhole as in a transverse (concert) flute. The second has a whistle-type reed, as in a recorder. The first is simple to make, but the second is far easier to play.

The basic form of the clay ocarina can be coiled or pinched in two halves and later joined to form the sound chamber, but for speed and convenience the technique shown here is that of press moulding with rolled out slabs of clay.

The ocarina body

The early stages are the same for either form.

You will need:

About 375gm (12oz) prepared earthenware or stoneware clay.

Rolling pin.

Guide sticks about 6mm ($\frac{1}{4}$″) thick.

Sharp knife.

Small wire loop tool for drilling the finger holes (each about 6mm ($\frac{1}{4}$″) in diameter).

A short piece of hacksaw blade.

A banding wheel, or card templates.

Two shallow plaster moulds, which can be bought, made (Clay chapter 13, page 538) or improvised from cereal bowls.

☐ Roll out an oblong slab of clay large enough to provide two discs, which should be between 8cm and 13cm (3″ and 5″) across.

☐ Cut the slab in half to produce two square slabs.

☐ Cut two discs, either by placing the clay on a banding wheel and cutting with the sharp knife (fig.1) or by using card templates. Always make one disc slightly larger than the other as this facilitates joining.

☐ Press the discs carefully into shallow concave plaster moulds.

☐ Leave the discs, or domes as they are now, to become firm but not dry.

☐ Mix a small amount of slip, about half a cupful, from some of the remaining clay.

☐ When the domes are firm enough to hold their shape, remove them from the moulds.

☐ Place the domes together, edge on edge, and note where they touch. As they do not fit flush together, some trimming is necessary.

☐ Use the hacksaw blade to score the two edges to be joined.

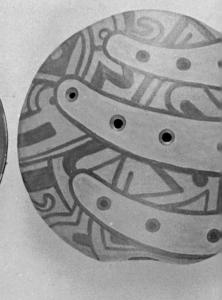

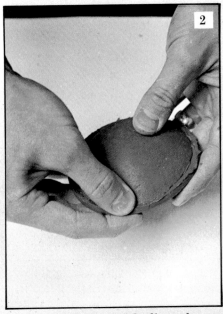

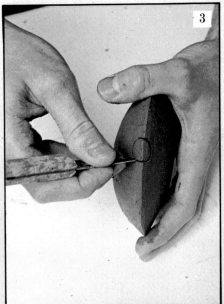

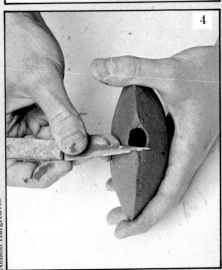

Nelson Hargreaves

□ Coat both edges with slip and carefully press the domes together, ensuring that slip oozes out all around the seam (fig.2).

□ Lightly score the edge of what is now a discus form, and round off smoothly to merge the two pieces of clay firmly together in an oval shape. It is now necessary to cut the blowhole, and so by this stage you must have decided which type of ocarina you want to make.

Side-blown ocarina. Cut a hole about 14mm ($\frac{1}{2}$") in diameter, so that it straddles the edge of the discus form (fig.3). This hole should be well rounded.

□ Bevel the two shoulders, each side of the hole (fig.4). The side-blown ocarina is now shaped.

South American designs inspired the subtle colours and patterns of these ocarinas and flutes by Neil Ions. Flutes are the subject of the next chapter.

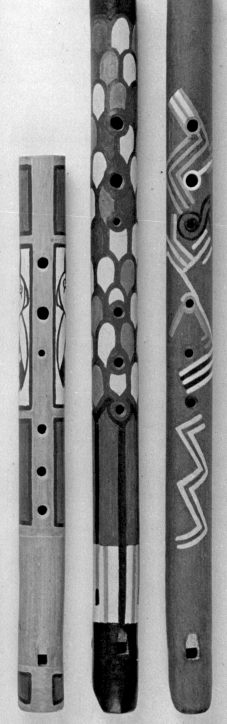

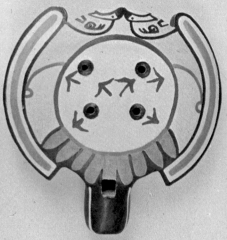

Paul Kemp

1879

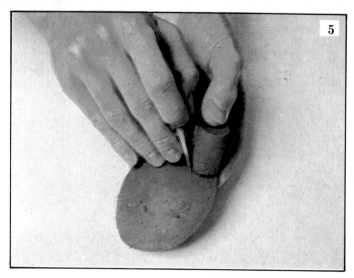

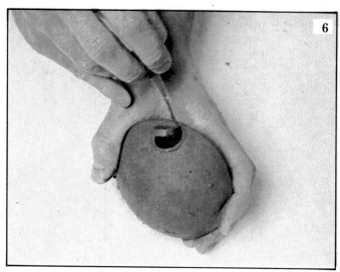

Whistle ocarina. Roll a coil 4cm (1¾″) long with a diameter of 2.5cm (1″).
□ Hold the coil directly below the edge of the sound chamber and use the point of the knife to mark, very lightly, where it lies (fig.5).

□ Cut a blowhole slightly smaller than the diameter of the coil, within the mark (fig.6).

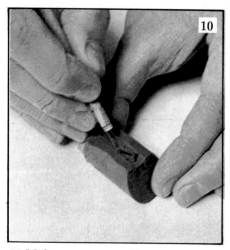

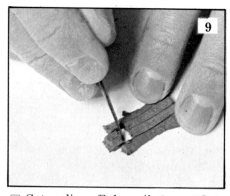

The reed

The reed is necessary for the whistle ocarina and also for the flutes which are the subject of the next chapter.
When the coil is firm, construct the whistle reed in the following manner.
□ Cut one end of the coil to fit the curve of the ocarina.
□ Hold the coil in position over the blowhole and mark a line down the coil's centre, from the point where it meets the ocarina body.
□ Mark a line each side of the central one, 6mm (¼″) apart (fig.7).

□ Cut a slice off the coil, 3mm (⅛″) in from, and at right angles to, the centre line (fig.8).
□ Cut out a 6mm (¼″) square notch between the marked lines, at the end of the slice which will touch the body, or sound chamber (fig.9).

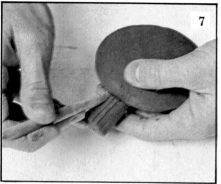

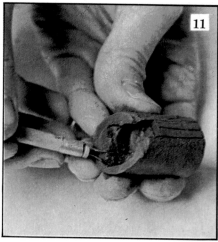

□ Make a corresponding groove 2mm (1/10″) deep along the centre of the flat surface of the coil (fig.10).
□ Replace the slice onto the coil, using a little slip. Make sure that the resulting slot does not become blocked with slip.
□ Use the wire loop tool to hollow out the end of the coil, directly behind the square notch (fig.11).

□ Holding the now completed reed in position over the blowhole, mark two short lines on the body from the edges of the notch. Bevel the blowhole between these lines at an angle of 30°.
□ Join the whistle to the sound chamber, first scoring and coating both edges with slip.
□ Blow the whistle while the join is still soft in order to find the correct alignment of the whistle to the sound chamber. This is crucial for the production of a good note. Adjust the join if necessary.
Remember that it is essential to achieve an airtight and strong join.
□ Bevel and shape the mouthpiece, however you choose, to form a comfortable shape for the lips, or to complement the design. For instance, in the case of the turtle ocarina the mouthpiece was shortened and curved to form a realistic head.

Paul Kemp

Finger holes

These can now be bored, with the aid of a wire loop tool, anywhere across one side of the sound chamber except very close to the blowhole. Each hole should be about 6mm ($\frac{1}{4}$") in diameter. You should familiarize yourself with the playing position of the instrument, in order to choose the most comfortable placings for the finger holes. Remember that the side-blown ocarina is played by blowing across the large hole and therefore the instrument is held roughly at right angles to the lips.

Up to five or six finger holes are usual on ocarinas of this type, but the number really depends a great deal on the accuracy of the whistle construction, the refinement of the side-blown hole and, of course, on your own blowing technique. If the first sounds are peculiar the player may be as much at fault as the instrument.

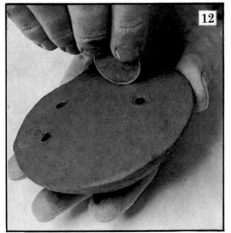

Use a small coin to countersink the finger holes so that the fingers can find them more easily. Place the edge of the coin on the hole and twist it gently (fig.12).

Above: slabs of clay attached to the whistle ocarinas give added interest to the form. Designed by Neil Ions.

Decoration

The instruments are now complete and can be decorated. Small coils or slabs of clay can be joined to the body to add sculptural interest to the form. An obvious choice would be to create a little bird as the Italians do.

The surfaces can be treated with incised or painted decoration, with coloured slips, underglaze paints, and glazes. When glazing, be sure that the holes remain unblocked, otherwise tuning may change or sound quality be impaired.

The examples shown here were painted with coloured slips which were allowed to dry and then burnished before firing. Finally, after firing, they were polished with ordinary wax furniture polish.

Making a zoetrope

The zoetrope was invented during the 19th century as a result of scientific study of objects in motion. The discovery of a way of seeing images move, by viewing a series of pictures representing phases of motion, gave rise directly to the invention of the zoetrope, which means 'wheel of life'. Out of this study also came the first moving pictures projected on to a screen. The zoetrope was the forerunner of these motion pictures and is therefore part of the tradition of the cinema.

The zoetrope was a popular parlour toy with Victorian children. Bands of drawings of clowns, jugglers or frisking animals were brought to life when viewed through the slits of a rotating cylinder. The same figure is drawn repeatedly with slight variations, so that it appears to move when the sequence of drawings is viewed in quick succession. The same simple principle is behind both the zoetrope and the modern cartoon film, though the latter is of course far more sophisticated.

A zoetrope is very simple to make. A number of connecting scenes, for example of a man running, are drawn along a strip of paper which is folded round in a circle and placed inside a cylinder with slits in the sides. The cylinder is then rotated, and an observer looking through the slits sees what is apparently a man running vigorously.

To make a zoetrope
You will need:
A strip of thin cardboard 12.5cm x 62cm (5" x 24½").
Thick cardboard, at least 91.5cm x 91.5cm (36" x 36").
Strips of cartridge paper 60cm x 6.25cm (24" x 2½"), as many as you wish, according to the number of picture sequences you wish to make.
Ruler.
Pencil and rubber.
Scalpel.
Pair of compasses.
Paint, crayons or felt-tipped pen.
A piece of balsa wood measuring 6mm x 6mm (¼" x ¼") across the top and 10cm (4") long.
General-purpose glue, such as PVA.
Record player (optional).

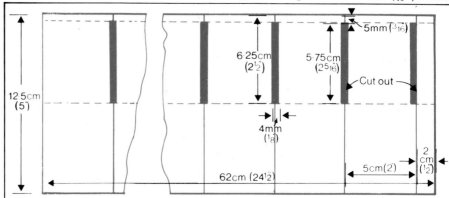

1. Pattern for the cylinder of a zoetrope. The slits are the viewing holes.

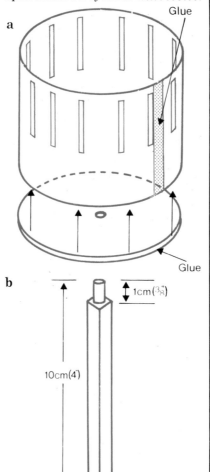

2. Assembling the cylinder and base upon which the cylinder will revolve.

To make the cylinder, take the strip of thin card and draw a pencil line lengthways along the card 6.25cm (2½") from each long edge. This divides card into two equal parts (fig.1). Draw another line the length of the card 5mm (³⁄₁₆") from the top (see fig.1).

☐ Draw pencil lines the width of the strip at intervals of 5cm (2"), leaving 2cm (½") at one end as shown. This will give you 12 pencil lines along the strip.

☐ Draw a pencil line 2mm (¹⁄₁₆") either side of each pencil line just marked, between the long horizontal lines except for the one 2cm (½") from the end of the card. For this one only, draw a line 4mm (⅛") to one side leaving the last 2cm (½") whole (see fig.1).

☐ Cut out these pieces with the scalpel so that you have 12 slots in the top half of the strip, each measuring 4mm x 5.75cm (⅛" x 2⁵⁄₁₆").

☐ Fold the strip round to form a cylinder. Apply glue to the last 2cm (½") of each end and stick these together.

☐ On the thick cardboard draw, with the pair of compasses, two circles each with a radius of 9.7cm (3⅞"). Put one aside for the base.

☐ With the scalpel, cut a small hole about 3mm (⅛") diameter in the centre of the first circle. (This will later take the balsa wood on which it will revolve.)

☐ Apply glue round the edge of this cardboard circle and fix it to the base of the cylinder (fig.2a).

To make the base, pare down to a dowel shape the top 1cm (³⁄₈") of the balsa wood with the scalpel (fig.2b), so that it fits loosely into the hole of the first circle.

☐ Glue the square base of the balsa wood stick to the centre of the second circle.

☐ On another piece of cardboard, draw four squares, each measuring 9cm x 9cm (3½" x 3½").

A Victorian zoetrope with its collection of drawings. The circular designs fit the base.

1833

□ Open a pair of compasses to 8cm (3¼″), place the point in the top right-hand corner of one square and draw an arc (fig.3). Repeat with the other four squares.

□ Cut out and keep the four L-shaped pieces. Glue these to the balsa wood and base, as supports for the stick which will support the cylinder (fig.4).

□ Using the compasses, draw and cut out another circle of thick card with a radius of 5cm (2″).

□ Cut a hole in the centre for the balsa wood to go through.

□ Apply glue to the top of the four supports, push the circle over the balsa wood and stick it on the supports (fig.5).

□ Place the cylinder on the base, with the balsa wood going through the hole in the centre of the cylinder. (Do not use glue.)

To make the pictures, first cut a piece of cartridge paper 60cm x 6.25cm (24″x 2½″).

□ Draw pencil lines at 5cm (2″) intervals along the strip, dividing it

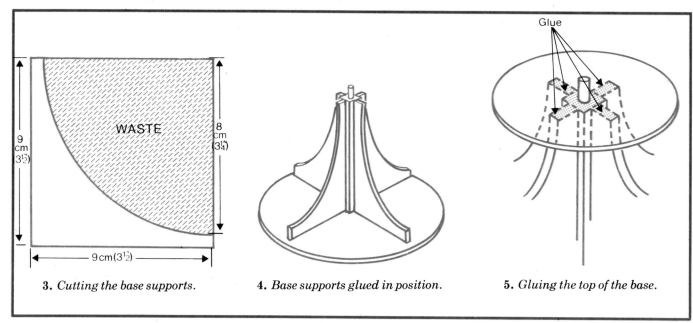

3. *Cutting the base supports.*

4. *Base supports glued in position.*

5. *Gluing the top of the base.*

6. *These drawings are two sequences showing 'frozen' moments in the course of playing and dancing. When revolved in a zoetrope each sequence becomes animated.*

Trevor Lawrence

into 12 equal parts for the drawings.

☐ Trace off the drawings of either of the sequences shown (fig.6) or devise your own drawings. Remember that to be effective the sequences must show progressive action.

☐ Draw them on to the strip, one to a section. Repeat them in the sequence 1, 2, 3, 4, 3, 2, 1, 2, 3, 4, 3, 2, from left to right, until you have filled the strip. (If you are going to place the zoetrope on a revolving record player as described here, they should be drawn from right to left.) Colour them in and rub out the pencil lines between them. (You can build up a collection of different strips of drawings.)

To assemble, place the strip inside the cylinder, resting it on the bottom and round the sides.

☐ Spin the cylinder by hand or place it on a revolving record player and look through the slits: you will see a moving image.

Drawings appear to 'come to life' in an easily operated zoetrope.

Sandra Lousada

Tanning and dressing fur

Among early man's basic needs in cold climates was warmth and soon after he learned to use animals for food he discovered that their pelts, after special treatment, could be used for clothing. This treatment involved drying, curing and softening pelts by beating them with a stick.

Good furs are now a much treasured commodity and their prices put them out of the reach of many people. But there is no reason why skins cannot be successfully tanned at home much as they were in early times.

The results should not be expected to compare in appearance and pliability with products of a commercial tannery or factory, so it would be unwise to begin with a visit to a mink farm, but if you live in the country or have farmer friends you may have access to rabbit, fox or even mole or squirrel skins. If not, a butcher who specializes in game or a poulterer may help— some butchers are often pleased to sell skins for a modest sum as they will probably have no other outlet for them.

Selecting skins

Whatever the type of skin, it is most important to deal with it as soon as possible after the animal has died— once the natural decomposition begins, nothing can rectify the damage or replace fallen hair or fur. If you are buying skins from a butcher, remember to collect them as soon as possible.

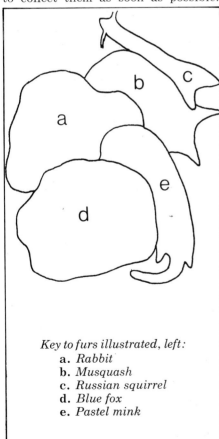

Key to furs illustrated, left:
  a. *Rabbit*
  b. *Musquash*
  c. *Russian squirrel*
  d. *Blue fox*
  e. *Pastel mink*

When choosing skins, watch out for moult (shedding) as the fur from a moulting skin will always tend to 'slip' —that is to drop out. A few moult spots on the belly will not matter as these can be avoided when cutting out but moult patches on the back of the skin will limit the amount of usable fur.

Look, too, for pellets in the skin—the pellets will, of course, leave damaging holes.

Where to work

It is essential to work near a water supply—a garage or outhouse that is near one is ideal. However, as long as you protect your working surfaces with plenty of newspaper and provided you keep all materials away from food it is possible to work in the kitchen.

The amount of space and equipment available may limit the number of skins you can cope with at one go as there are various stages where the skins need to be left flat to dry. It is advisable, therefore, to begin with only a few small skins. Once you know your limits, you can match up a whole batch of skins which are intended for a particular item.

Preparing skins

It is wise to over-estimate slightly the number of skins required in case any get damaged in the tanning process. Once you have obtained your skins you can start tanning immediately, but a better end result will be achieved if the skins are either dried or salted first. Because of the space and equipment necessary for proper drying, salting is the most suitable method for home use.

Salting. Open out the pelt and remove any lumps of flesh or dirt with a blunt knife, but do not use any water at this stage. Make quite sure that all fat is removed.

Lay the pelt out flat, fur side down, on a board and cover with a thick layer— up to 6mm ($\frac{1}{4}$″)—of common salt. The pelt can be stretched and tacked on the board, but this is optional. Store in a cool, dark place for a couple of weeks or longer if it is not convenient to start tanning. You could put a barrier of moth-balls around the skin to help keep insects away from the fur.

Liquid will begin to ooze from the skin and stain the salt but this is quite normal. Make sure that the surface of the skin remains completely covered by a layer of salt. Once pelts have dried out, they may be stored in boxes for a short time but always store leather to leather and fur to fur as the slightest amount of grease on the fur will cause damage.

Cleaning. After salting or drying, the pelts must always be thoroughly washed in many changes of clean cold water. If a pelt has been salted or dried,

then it will need a really thorough soaking for at least twelve hours— possibly as long as two days, depending on the size and thickness of the skin. When the skin is soft and flexible, lay it on a board or over a pole, fur side down, and work over the flesh side with a blunt blade—such as an old table knife—to break up and remove any remaining tissue, flesh or fat. Rub the blade back and forth against the skin. At the same time, work the grease and oil out of the skin. If the skin still appears to be greasy it can be worked with the blade in a solution of lukewarm water containing 25gm (1oz) washing soda to 5 litres (9 pints) water and then rinsed again thoroughly in clean water. Leave the skin on a tilted surface (fig.1) for surplus moisture to drain off. The pelt is now ready for tanning.

1. *Pelt is drained on tilted board.*

Tanning

There are several ways of tanning skins. The directions which follow are two of the more successful home methods—the first method, using salt and sulphuric acid, although more complicated, generally gives a better result.

Salt and acid tanning
You will need:
Rubber gloves.
Large apron or overall.
Large container—an old tin or enamel bath or a sound wooden barrel would be ideal.
Wooden broom handle or piece of thick dowelling for stirring.
Large boards where pelts can be left for a period of time without disrupting domestic routine.
Large quantity of common cooking salt.
90ml (3fl oz) dilute sulphuric acid—as used for car batteries and available from most garages.
Potash alum or ammonium alum— obtainable from most chemists (optional).
Washing soda (optional).

□ In your container, prepare a solution of 1kg (2lb) common cooking salt in 9 litres (15 pints) of water. To this add 90ml (3fl oz) of dilute sulphuric acid. This quantity will tan six rabbit skins so increase or decrease the amounts according to the size and number of pelts.

□ Mix the solution thoroughly and immerse the pelts making sure there is sufficient liquid to completely cover them.

□ Leave for 24 hours, stirring and agitating with a stick from time to time. Some large or thick pelts may take a few hours longer.

□ To test that a pelt is thoroughly soaked, cut a small test area from an edge and check that it is white and opaque throughout its thickness.

□ Allow to drain by laying out in a safe place, where the dripping moisture can do no harm, or place on a wooden board set at an angle with one end resting in a container so that all the surplus liquid drains back into it. This solution may be re-used but will probably need to be strained first to remove any particles of fur, skin etc. The skin may now be dressed but a softer, more pliable pelt can be achieved with one further treatment.

□ Prepare a solution of 500gm (1 lb) common cooking salt in 9 litres (15 pints) of water with 1kg (2lb) of potash alum or ammonium alum. Keep adding small doses of a strong solution of washing soda to this until the cloudiness produced at first just ceases to dissolve with vigorous stirring—that is until a saturated solution has been formed.

□ Leave the pelt in this solution for at least 24 hours, stirring frequently, then drain as before.

Formalin method

This method may suit your available facilities better. It is quicker than, though not quite so good as the previous method.

You will need:

Rubber gloves, apron, broom handle and large boards as for first method.

Large container—in this case it could be plastic.

Formalin—obtainable from most chemists.

□ Prepare a solution of 5% formalin—you can buy it already diluted to 5% but it is usually less expensive to buy full strength formalin and dilute it yourself. Use one part formalin to 20 parts water—take care not to inhale the fumes. Make up sufficient solution to cover the pelts completely and allow

them to move easily when stirred.

□ Leave pelts in solution for up to one week, preferably in a well ventilated

Sandra Lousada

outhouse, stirring from time to time. Small skins may not need a week but test first as described for the first

The positioning of pelts in this rabbit coat gives a striking symmetry of pattern. Rabbit is inexpensive, but can produce exciting results.

A sumptuous wolfskin bedspread for warm nights and self-indulgent luxury.

David Levin

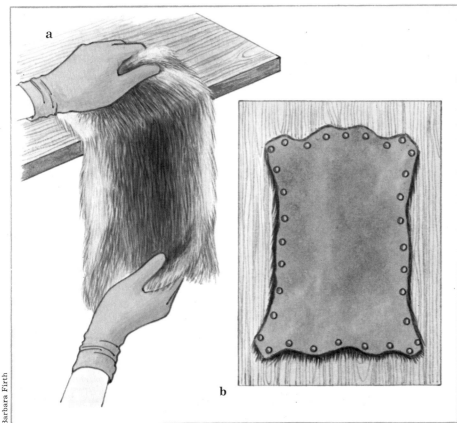

Barbara Firth

2. Two stages in dressing skin: it is softened over a board and nailed out to dry.

method using salt and acid.

☐ Rinse the pelts really thoroughly—if possible under a trickling water supply for two days, otherwise in a large container with plenty of changes of clean cool water. Then allow to drain as before.

Dressing

Whichever method you choose for tanning the skins, the dressing procedure is the same.

You will need:

2 egg yolks—without a trace of white. Neat's-foot oil or cod-liver oil. Boards, nails, brushes and sandpaper.

After the pelt has been drained or gently squeezed as dry as possible, it should be smoothed out evenly on a flat surface with flesh side uppermost. Beat the raw egg yolks and mix well with twice their volume of neat's-foot oil or cod-liver oil. The quantity given here will dress six rabbit skins.

☐ Apply a thin layer to flesh side of pelt and leave for a day to dry slowly.

☐ While the pelt is drying, work it from time to time with your hands to soften it—stretch it in all directions and work the flesh side over the edge of a board, pulling it backwards and forwards as if polishing shoes with a cloth (fig.2a). If the skin is rough, smooth it by working over a sandpaper block which also helps to make it soft and pliable. Much of the success in producing a soft, pliable skin depends upon this repeated working which must be done while the skin is drying out—not after it is dry.

☐ If the pelt appears to be drying out rather hard or brittle, it may be necessary to moisten the flesh side with a brush dipped in water and apply more dressing mixture, stretching and pulling the skin as before.

☐ Before the pelt dries completely, lay it fur side down on a large board and smooth it out flat, stretching it slightly from the centre outwards.

☐ Fix pelt to the board with nails (fig.2b). Any traces of dried salt on the fur side can be removed by brushing and beating the skin side of the pelt with a stick as you would a carpet.

Your pelts are now ready to be made up into fashion garments, accessories or toys. Instructions for sewing fur and suggestions for their use are given in the following chapters.

Safety

Sulphuric acid must be kept in a clearly labelled glass container and not left lying about as all acids are dangerous. Be very careful when working and, if you splash your clothes, wash it off immediately as the acid burns.

Tongue and groove wall panelling

Natural timber panelling can be used to decorate any room in a house. The different wood grains provide a wide range of colours and patterns and, since timber is hard wearing, re-decorating problems will be minimized.

Most woods can be used for decorating interiors. The choice of timbers, therefore, should depend on cost, availability and appearance. Many softwoods are very pale in colour while hardwoods range from the creamy yellow of ash, beech or sycamore to the richer browns of mahogany, cherry and walnut.

When choosing a wood for timber panelling, it is important to consider the moisture content of the wood; timber which has a high water content will shrink and warp in a heated room. Always ask the advice of the wood merchant when purchasing.

Tongue and groove—'T and G'—wood panels are most commonly used for internal wall claddings as the interlocking joints allow for easy assembly. Different lengths of panel are available to fit the height of an average room. However, if you want horizontal panelling, you may find that the panels need to be joined end-to-end.

Timber

Panels are between 10mm and 19mm ($\frac{3}{8}''$ and $\frac{3}{4}''$) thick and 75mm to 150mm (3" to 6") wide. The thickness determines both the rigidity of the panelling and the spacing of the battens.

10mm ($\frac{3}{8}''$) panels are recommended for all internal wall linings as they are light weight and easy to handle in construction.

Allowance for movement of the panels, due to contraction and expansion, is made when the tongues and grooves are originally machined (fig.1).

The choice of panelling depends on the shape and use of the room, its size and lighting, and on personal choice. Factors which should be taken into account are: the extent of coverage desired, what kind of wood to use and the angle at which to fix the panels.

Another consideration is your own skill. Covering a whole room, and even a whole wall, involves a range of technical problems. Unless you are an experienced woodworker it is recommended that large walls, especially with doors or windows in them, be avoided. Many smaller areas can be enhanced by panelling and are easier to do.

Preparations

The method of fixing the panels depends primarily upon the type and area of the wall you intend covering.

Before fixing any panels to new walls be sure the walls are dry. Newly plastered walls take at least two months to dry before panels can be safely fixed to them.

Masonry walls such as unfaced or plastered bricks or lightweight building blocks—eg breezeblock—will need a timber framework of battening attached directly to their surfaces. The tongue and groove panels are then fixed to these (fig.2).

Walls constructed with a timber framework will also need battens unless the vertical and horizontal wooden members in the wall are close enough to make battens unnecessary.

You can locate these wooden members by using a bradawl at intervals across, and up and down, the walls. The bradawl has a steel blade with a flat point, like a chisel, and is used mainly for 'boring' small holes in softwood. Make a pencil mark every time you strike solid timber; you will eventually be able to rule a grid pattern on the wall, showing exactly where the members are.

Wiring and plumbing

Take care when drilling not to pierce any electrical wiring or pipework. Remove light fittings from the wall to be covered, and check where the wire enters the fitting. If it enters at the top do not drill or nail into any area of wall directly above the fitting. Similarly for wires coming in from the side—do not drill anywhere along a horizontal line from the fitting to the edge of the wall.

Damp-proofing

If the wall to be panelled has a tendency to dampness or will be subject to condensation—as it would in a bathroom or kitchen—you may prevent this from affecting the panelling by treating both the battens and the boards with a clear wood preservative. This will protect the timber from damp, fungal and insect attack.

Insulation

If necessary you can insulate against heat and sound by inserting a layer of thick, flare-free expanded polythene sheeting, glass fibre, or mineralized rock-wood quilting between the wall surface and the panelling. This should only be necessary if large areas are covered.

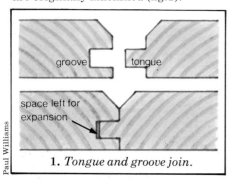

groove / tongue

space left for expansion

Paul Williams

1. Tongue and groove join.

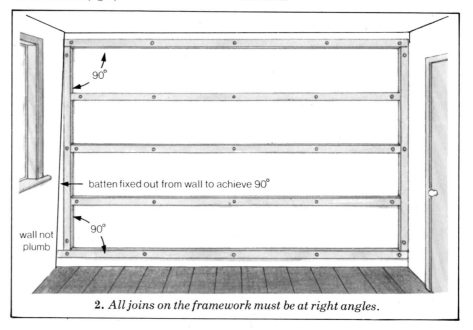

90°

batten fixed out from wall to achieve 90°

wall not plumb

90°

2. All joins on the framework must be at right angles.

ZEFA

Battens

Estimating the amount of wood needed for the battens is a fairly simple procedure. Battens are constructed from softwood and should be bought in lengths to fit the area you wish to cover.

You will need:

50mm x 25mm (2″ x 1″) softwood—length and number according to size of wall covered and number of battens required.

5cm (2″) No.10 masonry screws (if fixing to such a wall) and fibre or plastic proprietary wall plugs.

6.2cm (2½″) flathead nails—for use, if necessary, on a timber framework wall.

Electric drill and high speed masonry bit or Rawlplug tool.

Spirit level for both vertical and horizontal measurement.

The battens must present a plane (flat) surface for the panelling to fit over evenly. However, it is not necessary to go to great lengths to achieve a level surface as neither walls nor timber are ever perfectly true. Major irregularities in a wall can be corrected by packing the battens with scraps of wood to get the correct level, or by shaping a batten, with a Surform tool or plane, to fit over a 'high spot'.

Masonry walls. Battens are fixed to masonry walls with 5cm (2″) No.10 masonry screws with fibre or plastic proprietary wall plugs.

An electric drill, set to run at a slow speed and fitted with a high-speed masonry bit or Rawlplug tool for tapping holes may be used on concrete or very hard brick walls.

You can use masonry nails (not less than 6cm (2½″) long) to fix battens to lightweight building blocks such as breezeblock.

Fixing the battens. If covering a whole wall, begin by removing the skirting boards and protruding ceiling moulds.

Sloping wall covered with T and G panels. The angle of the wall makes the covering more difficult.

☐ Next, a 'frame' of battening is put up round the wall or around the area to be covered (see fig.2). Begin by fixing a horizontal batten across the top of the wall, 5cm (2″) down from the ceiling. If the panelling only reaches, say half way up the wall, then the top batten must be exactly at the height of the panels. With the spirit level check that it is reasonably level before fixing permanently in place.

☐ Fix a second horizontal batten about 7.5cm (3″) up from the floor, checking with the spirit level that it is straight.

☐ Cut two vertical battens to fit between the horizontals. These should go at the ends of the wall or area to be covered. Before fixing them permanently, check with the spirit level held vertically that the wall is plumb, ie straight up and down. If the wall is out of plumb, bring each batten into plumb by fixing it (or one end of it) slightly out from the end of the wall. Ensure that the vertical and horizontal frames meet at 90° (see fig.2).

Once the frame is completed, you need only to fill in the intermediate spaces with battens.

Battens should be fixed 45cm to 60cm (18″ to 24″) apart measuring from the centre of one batten to the centre of the other. The thicker the panels the greater the distance between battens. Fix the battens counter to the direction intended for the panelling. Keep the battens reasonably level or plumb, as straight battening will make nailing easier when you come to fix the panels.

Fixing the panels

There are three important points to note when fixing panels: first, where possible, always begin panelling from a corner to avoid waste and to establish a 'true' panel so that the following panels can be joined on correctly and do not 'stagger' out of line.

Second, 'square off' the first panel with the adjoining wall and ceiling before nailing, as few ceilings and walls are straight.

Third, leave a 6mm (¼″) gap between the panelling and the floor and ceiling for air to circulate freely behind—this gap also allows the panels to expand slightly in damp or humid atmospheres.

You will need:
T and G panels, preferably 10mm (⅜″) thick—sufficient to cover required area.

3.2cm (1¼″) rust-proofed lost-head nails —for fixing panels.

Nail punch, wood filler and fine grade glasspaper.
Chisel, hammer, saw and plane.

Scribing. If the wall is slightly curved, it may be necessary to trim your first panel to fit exactly into a corner.

To do this hold the panel against the corner, flush to the butting wall and the ceiling. Use the spirit level to get the panel straight. The exact contour of the wall is then traced on to the panel with a pencil held against a small block of wood (fig.3). The panel is then trimmed along this line.

This is known as scribing and its advantage over measuring is that any unevenness in a surface will automatically be transferred in outline to the piece being traced.

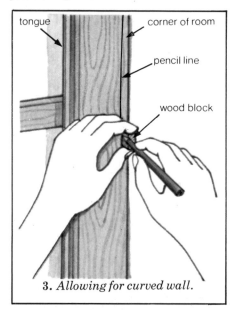

3. *Allowing for curved wall.*

Trim the edge of the panel with a fine set plane and sand with glasspaper.

Vertical panelling. Begin at a corner of the room (if possible). Scribe the grooved side of the first panel to fit into corner. Remember to leave a gap at the ceiling and floor for air to circulate.

☐ Keeping this panel plumb, begin nailing about 6mm (¼″) away from the corner or edge, using 3.2cm (1¼″) lost-head nails.

The nails should be driven at a 45° angle into the batten work behind—this is known as 'skew pinning'. Use a nail punch to push the nail below the surface of the panel. Work down the panel, pinning into the corresponding battens. Fill holes with filler.

☐ On the other side of the panel, place nails along the tongue of the panel and skew pin at 45° (inset fig.4). Sink the nails using a nail punch.

☐ Fit the groove of the next board over the tongue, thereby hiding the nail heads.

☐ Part drive nails into the tongue of this panel. Working from the top down, cramp the panel up close to the preceding one using a chisel and waste wood (see fig.4), and drive nails home. Use the nail punch to sink them.

Cramping should always be done on the tongue side of the panel, so that the next board can hide any marks. It is necessary to cramp tightly to prevent openings appearing at the joints when the timber shrinks.

☐ When you come to the third panel, cramp and nail from the bottom up instead of from the top down—cramping always in the same order will gradually skew the boards out of line. When you reach the last two or three boards to be fixed along a wall and into a corner, do not cramp them. Instead, cut the last a little oversize (fig.5a) and fit boards together so they make a bowed shape (fig.5b). The boards are sprung into position (fig.5c) and nailed fast, the holes being filled with wood filler.

If the top and bottom edges of the vertical panelling are uneven after being fixed, a narrow skirting board or beading can be fitted. Fix with panel pins (length according to the thickness of the skirting or beading), nailing through to the panels. Skirting board for the ceiling should be fitted upside down.

Remember that if the room is very humid or damp—eg the kitchen or bathroom—then a gap must be left for ventilation purposes.

Horizontal panelling. This is fixed in a similar way to the vertical panels.
☐ Position the first board about 2cm (¾″) above the floor level with the tongue upwards.
☐ Check that it is level and skew pin through the surface of the panel about

Painted vertical T and G panels effectively enhance this corner of a room.

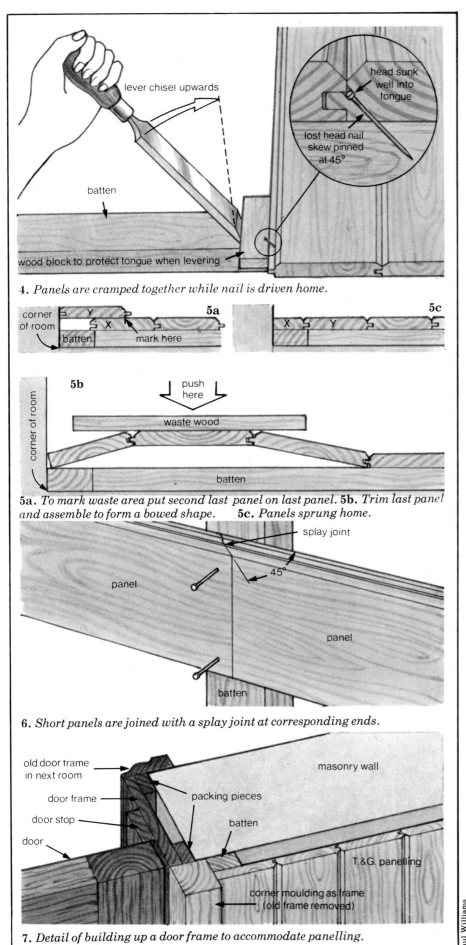

4. *Panels are cramped together while nail is driven home.*

5a. *To mark waste area put second last panel on last panel.* **5b.** *Trim last panel and assemble to form a bowed shape.* **5c.** *Panels sprung home.*

6. *Short panels are joined with a splay joint at corresponding ends.*

7. *Detail of building up a door frame to accommodate panelling.*

7cm (2¾″) up from the bottom edge of the panel.

☐ Next, skew pin along the edge of the tongue. The next panel will hide these nails.

☐ Continue fixing the panels up to the desired level, cramping each panel and checking with the spirit level. Remember to leave a 6mm (¼″) gap at ceiling level for air to circulate.

If you cannot buy panels which fit the entire length of the wall join them using the splay joint (fig.6).

Doors and windows

When fixing panelling around doors and windows it is important to see that the rough edges of the panels do not protrude beyond the wood surrounds of the doors or windows.

Usually the combined thickness of the battens and the panels is greater than the thickness of the window or door frames. The frames must therefore be removed in order to fit new ones of a suitable thickness. This is done before the panelling is fitted.

Pry off the existing frames being careful not to damage the wall or adjoining woodwork. Window sills can either be trimmed flush with the wall surface or removed completely.

Replace old frames (or, in the case of doors and windows without any frames, make new ones) with timber of the size required to build the frames up slightly thicker than the combined thickness of battens and panels (fig.7). Should you want to keep your existing frames, mount them on to the new frames. The new frame, in this case, must be just thick enough to enable the old frame to be built up to the correct level and of the same width as the original frame.

When putting up vertical panelling around a door, work across from corner to door, then across the wall space above the frame, and then across the wall on the opposite side of the door.

If panelling around a window, follow the same procedure, filling in the area underneath the window last. Scribe and cut boards to fit around corners of frames.

For horizontal panelling, begin on one side of the door and work up to the top of the frame, butting the boards against the frame as you go.

Work up the wall on the other side of the door in the same way. Finally, fix panels across the area above the frame. Do not place splay joints in the same place but stagger them or they will make an unsightly line.

For horizontal panelling around windows follow the same procedure. Begin at the bottom, working up and around either side of the window and then across the top.

Paul Williams

Traditional deep buttoning

When you have successfully re-upholstered a dining chair by traditional methods and have done some deep buttoning with foam padding, you could combine the techniques on a traditionally upholstered chair which has a deep-buttoned seat or back. The method for working the deep buttoning on these surfaces is very similar if the back is of a stuff-over style—where the stuffing is built up on the frame and the covering fabric is taken over the whole surface and tacked to the outside back. The method is different, however, on backs which have shallower, inset padding with a decorative border of wood round it. This is discussed in a later chapter.

The stuffing. In order to keep the cover fabric smooth between the buttons, the stuffing must be well packed which tends to make the surface rather hard. This can be counteracted by using a good-quality horsehair stuffing which has a lot of springiness even when firmly packed. Good-quality horsehair has long lengths of hair—15cm-20cm (6"-8") long—in comparison with the shorter lengths of cheaper hair.

You may find that your original stuffing was good horsehair in which case it is worth re-using it. You can restore its springiness by washing it in mild soapy water, rinsing it well and drying it in a warm place.

Materials and equipment
You will need:
Mallet and ripping chisel.
Webbing and webbing strainer.
Hessian, scrim, upholstery wadding.
Horsehair stuffing.
Twine.
Calico, cover fabric.
Button moulds.
Spring needle.
Double-pointed straight needle.
Improved and fine tacks; tack hammer.
Regulator; scissors.
Tailor's chalk.
Braid and adhesive such as Bostik 1 (for chairs with show-wood only).

Backs and unsprung seats
☐ Strip off the old cover fabric and, if the original surface was deep-buttoned, keep it as a guide to the amount of new fabric required. Allow about 10cm (4") extra all round for fitting.

☐ Examine the upholstery to see whether it needs replacing—if the hessian is in good condition and the scrim is not torn you may simply need to wash and tease out the second layer of horsehair stuffing, adding more if necessary. Then replace the calico and cover as described below. If the upholstery does need replacing, proceed as follows.

☐ Strip off the old upholstery as described in Upholstery chapter 3, page 468 (backs are stripped in a similar way to seats). Keep the scrim covering the first stuffing as a guide to the buttoning pattern.

☐ Start the new upholstery as described in chapter 3 and work the blind and top stitching as described in chapter 4, page 486. If you are working on a back follow the same principles as for a chair, using the original upholstery as a guide to the details.

The buttoning pattern. Make a template of the surface to be covered by holding a piece of paper against it and drawing round the edge.

☐ Find the centre point of each edge and draw lines across the template between the centre points on opposite edges. If the original surface was buttoned, measure the distance between the rows of buttons on the scrim (saved from the stripped upholstery) and draw a grid on the template to correspond.

If the old surface was not buttoned, start from the centre lines and draw a grid of parallel lines as described in Upholstery chapter 11, page 1870.

☐ Mark the positions for the buttons to form diamond shapes, leaving a clear border of about 5cm (2") all round.

Fabric template. Make a second template for the cover fabric, with the lines 4cm (1½") further apart as decribed in chapter 11. Remember to allow extra all round for the un-buttoned border and for the depth of the padding.

Victorian dining chair, re-upholstered with a horsehair-stuffed seat and a deep-buttoned velvet cover. The same techniques are used for chair backs or the arm rest of a chaise longue.

1895

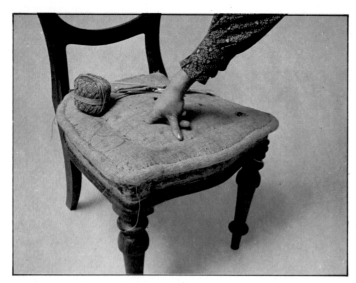

1. *At each button position insert an index finger into the stuffing through the hole cut in the scrim to ensure that the buttons sink deeply into the seat.*

2. *Making twine markers for each button position. The needle is passed through the stuffing to make a small stitch in the hessian below before being pushed back.*

3. *When the second stuffing has been applied, the twine markers, indicating the positions of the buttons, are pulled through it.*

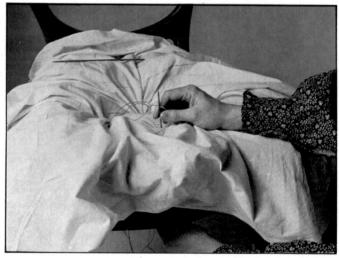

4. *Passing the needle through the calico and stuffing to the underside of the chair. The tail of twine on top is treated in the same way after making a small stitch.*

☐ Measure the template as a guide to the amount of calico and cover fabric required. (If the chair has other un-buttoned surfaces to be upholstered, use the old pieces of cover fabric as a guide to the fabric required.)

The second stuffing. Using tailor's chalk or ballpoint pen, transfer the markings from the buttoning template to the scrim covering the first stuffing. To make holes for the buttons to sink into the stuffing, cut a slit in the scrim at each button position and insert your index finger into the stuffing until you can feel the hessian below (fig.1).

☐ To make markers so you can find the button positions when the second stuffing is in position, thread the long needle with about 30cm (12″) of twine, pass it through the hole and stuffing and pull out underneath. Make a small stitch in the hessian and then push the needle back. Tie the ends of twine together. Repeat for each button

position (fig.2).

☐ Make bridle ties for the second stuffing and add this in the usual way. Pull through the markers (fig.3).

Calico cover. You may feel tempted to rush over this stage in eagerness to see the effect of the main cover—in fact this is one of the most important stages of the technique because it shapes the second stuffing into the mounds between the buttons, so take time and be patient.

☐ Transfer the markings of the button positions from the fabric template to the calico cover with tailor's chalk.

☐ Place the calico cover over the second stuffing and align the centre button positions. Press the calico down into the stuffing and into the hole in the scrim.

☐ Start at the centre button and work each diamond in turn. For each button, thread the straight upholstery needle with 30cm (12″) of twine. Insert the

needle into the calico, through the hole (fig.4) and bring it out on the reverse side (ie the underside of a seat or the outside back of a chair). Pull through, leaving a tail of twine of about 15cm (6″) on the calico.

☐ Unthread the needle and re-thread it with the 15cm (6″) tail. Insert the needle into the calico again, making a stitch of about 5mm (¼″). Pull through and unthread the needle.

☐ Tie the ends of twine on the reverse side in a slip knot and tighten the knot round a small roll made from a scrap of hessian or scrim to prevent the knot from pulling back through the stuffing (fig.5).

☐ Repeat this process at the remaining button positions of the diamond, neatening the fullness that forms between the stitches into pleats. On the backs of chairs the pleats should face downwards; on seats they should face the front edge.

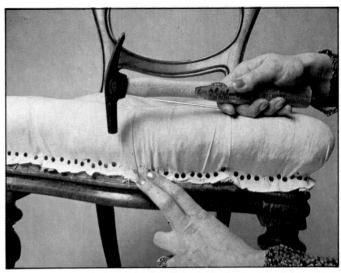

5. *Tightening the twine in a slip knot round a roll of scrim on the underside of the chair. The roll prevents the knot from pulling back through the stuffing.*

6. *Tacking down the calico, placing the tacks above the tack line of the cover. Notice how the fullness at the edge is formed into pleats on the straight grain.*

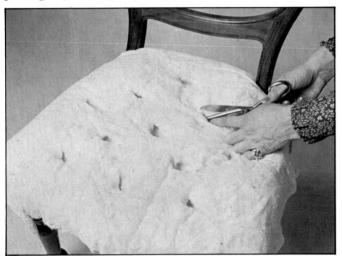

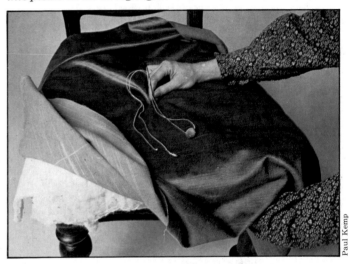

7. *Making slits in the wadding at each button position so the buttons on the cover can be pulled down firmly. Wadding prevents the horsehair from working through.*

8. *Attaching the main cover. The button is threaded on the twine first so that both ends of twine can be threaded in the needle and passed through the stuffing together.*

☐ Feel the mound of stuffing in the diamond: it should be firm and smooth. If it is flabby, poke some more stuffing into it with the flat end of the regulator and prod it with the pointed end until the shape is correct.

If the calico seems very taut and strained and you are likely to have trouble keeping the grain straight when you work the adjoining diamonds, it may be because there is too much stuffing in which case you should use the regulator to hook some out.

☐ Continue working in this way, completing each diamond at a time. Neaten the fullness at the edges into pleats which lie on the straight grain and tack down the calico, placing the tacks just above the tack line of the original cover (fig.6).

Main cover. Mark the wrong side of the cover fabric in the same way as for the calico. Use the remaining scraps of fabric to cover the button moulds.

☐ Cut a piece of wadding to cover the calico and place it, 'skin' side out, in position. Make a slit in the wadding at each button position but do not press it down into the holes (fig.7). There is no need to tack the wadding in position.

☐ Place on the cover fabric and start buttoning as for the calico. This time thread a button on the twine first so that both ends of twine can be threaded in the needle and passed through the fabric together (fig.8). Tighten the slip knot round the same roll as for the knots on the calico.

☐ Continue buttoning, keeping the grain of fabric absolutely square. Tack the cover to the frame along the tack line of the original cover and trim off the excess fabric. Cover with braid if required.

Sprung seats

These are deep buttoned in a similar way to unsprung seats except that the

twine is tied on the right side instead of the reverse side because of the springs.

☐ To make the stitch, insert the needle from the right side, leaving a tail of twine. As soon as the eye of the needle is through the hessian above the springs, push it back eye first, making a small stitch on the reverse side of the hessian. Insert the small roll of hessian or scrim into the stitch on the reverse side (this process may seem fiddly at first but you soon get the knack).

☐ Tie the ends of twine on the right side in a slip knot, threading the button on to one end of the second length used at the main cover stage. Pull the knot tightly.

☐ When all the button positions are stitched, cut the ends of twine leaving about 1.5cm ($\frac{1}{2}''$) on the length used on the calico stage but only 5mm ($\frac{1}{4}''$) on the length used on the main cover. Tuck the ends under the buttons.

Tinting prints by hand

Almost any uncoloured print can be made considerably more attractive by the addition of colour artistically applied. Since prints already have their subjects fully drawn, adding colour is an easy way for beginners to learn something about the use of colour and painting techniques in general.

History of tinting engravings

Nowadays meticulous hand-tinting of old engravings is only practised by a specialized few, but during the 18th and 19th centuries, publishers and print-sellers flourished with public demand for pictures; labour was cheap and attempts at producing quality art inexpensively resulted in the hand-colouring of monochrome prints. In the 1830s hand-colouring was the cheapest method of producing coloured prints, and lithographs were still being coloured by hand in the 1860s. Many subsequently famous artists, such as Turner, began their careers in this way, acquiring basic skill in handling brush and colour in the publishers' workrooms.

Between 1812 and 1821 there were also many penniless aristocratic refugees from the French Revolution only too happy to earn a few coins by colouring prints.

Some systems were more repetitive than creative, however. Artists would etch the original outlines on the copper plate and some would then colour a sample print in pale washes to be copied in quantity. The workers, many of them children, sat in a circle; each had a colour allotted to him, and brushed it on wherever it appeared in the guide copy; then he passed it to his neighbour for the next colour to be added. An edition of a book with many plates might require the hand-colouring of some 10,000 prints.

Obtaining engravings for tinting

Print shops and second-hand book-sellers are the best source of black and white engravings. Often these are not expensive and their condition is reasonably good.

Most engravings were printed as illustrations in books and some of the copies had tinted plates and were sold for more money.

If you wish to find out what colouring prints would have had if they had been tinted when published, a trip to the local library and antique print-sellers will be helpful. Museums are another place to find antique prints.

Preparation

Before colouring old engravings it is usually necessary to clean off the grime of a century or more.

Dry cleaning of loose surface dirt can be done with a ball of soft, slightly moist bread. A very soft eraser can be gently used on the margins and back, but never on the engraved surface.

Removing blemishes. Few antique prints will be completely free from the brown spots or blemishes known as 'foxing'. These are caused by exposure to pollution, smoke, damp, food crumbs, etc and must be removed by bleaching. Immerse the print in a shallow solution of sodium hypochlorite or common household bleach, diluted with water to the volume of one part bleach to twenty parts water. This is a very strong, quick acting solution; a print will need between one and three minutes' immersion to clean all but the heaviest foxing. Remember that when the print is wet it is very fragile, and any unsupported tugging will tear it. Rinse the print gently in clean water before leaving to dry on a flat hard surface.

Sizing. After drying, the print must be thoroughly sized to restore the strength of the paper, and to render it water-proof, so that traces of colour do not penetrate to the back.

Bottles of prepared jelly size can be bought in most art supply shops. This must be dissolved in warm water, one volume of size to three of water.

Alternatively, dissolve 1.5gm ($\frac{1}{4}$ tea-spoon) of household gelatine in a litre (2 pints) of hot water, and use immediately, brushing the solution across the surface of the print in broad flat strokes, in one direction only.

Right: begin colouring at the top of the print and work down. A flat wash of colour is all that is required, the engraver has already done the toning.

1899

Think not to find one meant Resemblance there   Prints should be prized as Authors should be read   A MIDNIGHT MODERN CONVERSATION   We sharply smile persuasive Folly dead   As Rabelais laught or as Cervantes Thought

We laugh the Vices but the Persons spare.   W.m Hogarth feat Price 3s 6d   As Nature dictated what Art has Taught.

Designed by W.m Hogarth   Engraved by T.C.ook

Think not to find one meant Resemblance there   Prints should be prized as Authors should be read   A MIDNIGHT MODERN CONVERSATION.   We sharply smile persuasive Folly dead   As Rabelais laught as Cervantes Thought

We laugh the Vices but the Persons spare.   or Nature dictated what Art has Taught.

Published Aprill the I 1796 by G.G.& J Robinson & John Nicholson Fleet Street London

1900

Colouring

To start colouring, practise on a print of little value. Use three or four good quality sable or camel-hair brushes ranging from sizes 2 to 4, for small octavo sized prints and sizes 8 to 10 for large folio prints, such as Hogarth's.

Keep to simple basic water colours—indigo, prussian blue, ultramarine, sepia, sienna, umber, light red, gamboge, ochre, olive green, viridian, payne's grey, naples yellow and a tube of chinese white (opaque).

Acrylic white gesso is also useful for underpainting highlights, such as on silk dresses which, when dry, can have transparent colour laid over it with great effect. This is also a good way of outlining a dark figure against a dark background.

Begin colouring at the top of the print —the sky if there is one.

Skies. Mix prussian blue with white or ultramarine very well diluted. It is much better to use very weak washes in the initial stages than to inadvertently use too strong a tone, which cannot be washed out. Remember you can always add more strength later if required, but cannot take it away. Try to finish a sky in one wash before it dries.

If you want to merge a pink cloud against a hazy blue background, first dampen area with clean water before using a mixture of raw sienna, light red and white. Naples yellow is also useful in skies.

Remember always that most of the toning work has already been done for you by the engraver, and that only flat washes of colour are required.

In a landscape keep your middle section and horizon as cool in colour as possible; use blues, greys and lavender, to obtain recession. Keep the warm tones, burnt sienna, ochre and light red for the bottom foreground. Do not waste your light areas by killing them with an opaque colour; keep them light with pretty transparent colours. Save the opaque colours for the dark details, highlighted with tiny touches of chinese white.

Buildings are pale washes of raw umber or ochre, brick is light red, slate roofs are payne's grey, cupolas, lime green.

Trees in the foreground are olive green lightened with ochre or gamboge, blueing to payne's grey and viridian in the distance.

Shadowed areas can be cool with blues, or warm with mauve or burnt sienna.

Figures and vehicles. Leave these until last. Bright spots of colour for

Left: Hogarth's 'A Midnight Modern Conversation', brought to life by careful but imaginative hand tinting.

mail coaches and carts, young ladies' dresses in light pinks and blues, older people in darker, more sedate colours.
Flesh tints are obtained by well-diluted light red with a touch of naples yellow, or for a more ruddy peasant complexion mix with burnt sienna. Opportunities for countless variations exist but remember the result must be

Graham Henderson

Making a collection of hand-tinted prints is an inexpensive way to add a 'connoisseur's touch' to your home.

colour harmony which is most easily achieved by restricting your basic colour palette. In this way your efforts may give both you and posterity the greatest of pleasure.

Latch-hooking on crochet

The magnificent coat in the photograph was made by hooking strands of yarn on to a crocheted foundation in the same technique used for hooked rugs made on canvas (Latch-hooking chapter 1, page 1110). The crocheted foundation, however, is softer and lighter and therefore more suitable for clothing.

Any oddments of knitting yarns can be used to make the pile surface so you may not necessarily have to buy much yarn, particularly if you unravel old knitted or crocheted garments. (The crimpiness of unpicked yarn from knitted garments gives the pile an unusual texture.)

This method can be used to make all forms of simply shaped garments, such as jackets, waistcoats, capes, gloves and hats or you could use it for cushions, rugs and coverlets. You could even rejuvenate old crocheted garments. The pile can be worked over the whole foundation or it could be used as a trimming only.

The foundation

The design. You can use any crochet pattern which is made in plain, closely worked treble or double treble stitches, or in filet crochet which is made by treble stitches separated by one chain stitch. Patterns for garments should be simple and loose fitting, and preferably worked on a large hook.

The yarn. Most yarns can be used for the foundation but, on a heavy garment such as a coat, it is best to make the foundation in a yarn which does not stretch—wool is usually better than synthetics. If you intend to work the pile over the whole foundation, it does not matter if you mix colours or dye lots provided you use the same type of yarn throughout.

The pile

Yarn. All kinds of knitting yarns can be used for the pile and it does not matter if you mix different types. The amount of yarn required will, of course, vary according to the garment being made, the length of the pile and the number of strands used in each knot. It is worth remembering that if you use a thick yarn the finished item will be very heavy—the coat in the photograph, for example, weighs about 3.17kg (7lb).

The lightest yarns to use are synthetics. Cotton yarns can also be used and these are particularly suitable for bath mats because they absorb moisture well.

Working the pile. Cut the strands of yarn for the pile following the method described in Latch-hooking chapter 1, page 1110.

Using either of the two methods for forming the knot described in the same chapter, work the knots on alternate stitches on foundations made in plain trebles or double trebles, and on every treble on foundations made in filet crochet.

Depending on the length of the pile and the number of strands used in each knot, the knots can be worked on every row on alternate rows—you will have to experiment in order to find the best effect.

*Left: strands of cotton yarn hooked on
a crocheted foundation make a soft
bath-mat. Designed by Liz Blackwell.
Right: different types of wool were
used for the pile of this coat,
designed by Shirley Anne Swayne.*

Peter Kibbles

How to draw shadows

Shadows can be used to great effect in painting and drawing, but to look convincing, they must be drawn correctly.

Light travels in straight lines, so when a ray of light meets an opaque object, the light cannot go round or through it and is either reflected or absorbed by the object. As a result a shadow is cast against whatever is behind the object. However, the shape and size of the cast shadow will not necessarily be the same as the object casting the shadow, but depends on several factors.

The light source. Light rays radiate from light sources such as the sun, light bulbs and candles, but because the sun is so far away, so few rays reach us that they are virtually parallel rather than radial. In fact all light rays from any very distant source such as the sun or moon are, in effect, parallel. In this chapter shadows cast by parallel light rays are discussed. Shadows cast by light from radiant sources are

dealt with in the next Design know-how chapter.

Fig.1 shows a drawing of a box with the sun fairly low on the horizon, slightly to the left-hand side. A shadow is cast by the box on the two sides nearest the observer. The size of the cast shadow has been determined by the following method.

☐ First draw the box and mark the vanishing points (see Design know-how chapter 62, page 1736).

☐ Determine and mark the sun and a point on the horizon line directly below the sun (point P). Lines drawn from the sun represent the light rays and angle of light which are parallel, but as they are drawn in perspective, they converge at a vanishing point, ie the sun. Lines drawn from point P represent the direction of the light rays, ie, north west of the box. These lines are also parallel, but are drawn in perspective and therefore converge at a vanishing point, ie point P.

☐ Following fig.1, through points A, B, C draw lines from the sun representing the angle of light.

☐ Through the points on the base of the box directly below the corners A, B and C, draw lines from point P to meet the lines drawn from the sun at points X, Y and Z.

☐ Join up points X, Y and Z with the corners below points A and C and you have drawn the outline of the shadow in perspective.

If your drawing is accurate, line XY will have the same vanishing point as line AB, and line YZ will have the same vanishing point as line BC.

This method of drawing shadows will work for a parallel light source at any angle. When the same box is drawn with a different light angle it will cast a different shadow.

Other factors will effect the shape and intensity of shadows. For example the surface on to which the shadow is cast will also effect the shape of the shadow. You will find that the same object casts different shadows depending on the surface behind it.

The intensity of the light will affect the intensity of the shadows. A dim light source, several different light sources or an overcast sky will all produce pale shadows, whereas one strong light source such as a spotlight or a bright sun will produce very strong shadows. So by lightening or darkening shadow intensity the comparative brightness of the day may be conveyed.

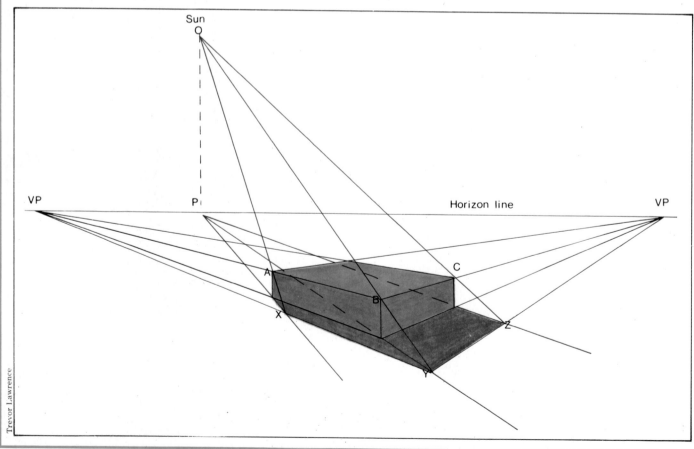

Trevor Lawrence